Current Trends and Traditions in Management Accounting Case Analysis

Fourth Edition

Gary Spraakman

CAPTUS PRESS

Current Trends and Traditions in
    Management Accounting Case Analysis, Fourth edition

Copyright © 1994, by Gary Spraakman and Captus Press Inc.
Copyright © 1995, 1998 by Gary Spraakman, Thomas Cheng
                and Captus Press Inc.
Copyright © 2001, by Gary Spraakman and Captus Press Inc.

First edition, first printing, Summer 1994
Second edition, first printing, Fall 1995
Third edition, Winter 1998
Fourth edition, Fall 2001

Captus Press Inc.
Mail: York University Campus
     4700 Keele Street
     North York, Ontario
     Canada   M3J 1P3
Telephone: (416) 736–5537
Fax: (416) 736–5793
Email: info@captus.com
Internet: http://www.captus.com

Canadian Cataloguing in Publication Data

Spraakman, Gary
     Current trends and traditions in management
accounting case analysis

4th ed.
Includes bibliographical references.
ISBN 1–55322–026–9

  1. Managerial accounting — Case studies.   I. Title

HF5657.4.S67 2001   658.15'11   C2001-902168-2

Canadä *We acknowledge the financial support of the Government
            of Canada through the Book Publishing Industry
Development Program (BPIDP) for our publishing activities.*

0 9 8 7 6 5 4 3 2 1
Printed in Canada

Table of Contents

I have many people to thank. My students deserve special thanks for allowing me to test these cases. I often learned more about the cases from their responses.

Specifically, I thank the following: Leslie Sanders for her editorial assistance with the first two sections of the casebook; The Society of Management Accountants of Canada for permission to adapt Lesson 1 of Management Processes and Problems (Course Code 553), September 1986 and the case, Jones Company, from their January 1983 Comprehensive Examination; Elizabeth Gayford for her response to the case, PC Board, Parts 1 and 2; and Simia Pir for her assistance with the cases, Yoour University and Electronic Process Equipment.

CHAPTER 1

Introduction

This book of cases is directed at students who are taking a course in management accounting. The materials presuppose an introductory course in accounting or financial accounting.

The book, intended to supplement management accounting textbooks, has six purposes. The first two are typical and related. They are: (1) to supply cases which demand the application of management accounting techniques, and (2) to introduce students to more practical situations than those typical of most textbooks. The next two purposes differentiate this case book from others: (3) to provide material that keeps abreast of changes to practice, and (4) to familiarize students with the traditions of case analysis in management accounting.

This collection responds to the difficulties our students experience when case analysis is demanded of them. I believe their difficulties occur for a number of reasons:

- Students spend up to 50 percent of their time reading and digesting the material before they do any thinking and writing. It is as if case authors advocate using long cases as teaching devices in order to allow adequate data for decision making, but the effort required to digest the case may leave the student little time for in-depth analysis.

- The case approach is learned, but not taught. Many students are forced to learn imprecisely the case approach in a very general and imprecise fashion, almost like osmosis.

- Although students can identify issues or problems, they have difficulty with analysis, i.e., they have trouble discerning related themes, causes, and effects, among issues, which is the objective of case analysis.

- Recommendations are readily suggested, but they are neither explained nor justified. When cases require implementation planning, it is outlined in the most rudimentary fashion.

- Case responses tend to display a superficial understanding of case questions. This is probably a result of the other weaknesses and not a separate weakness.

I believe these weaknesses have two roots. First, the teaching of the case approach is implicit. Case analysis skills appear elusive to students. Second, long, verbose cases encourage superficial thinking because there is insufficient time for in-depth considerations.

These weaknesses, and my desire to remove them, suggest the final two purposes of this collection: (5) to provide short cases so as to minimize reading time and to encourage greater depth of analysis, and (6) explicitly to teach case analysis and provide feedback for learning.

This is an exciting time in which to design a management accounting casebook. Management accounting is in a period of transition. Some, for example Johnson and Kaplan (1987), even argue that traditional management accounting is no longer relevant. These trends in management accounting are central. First, manufacturing, the sector that once dominated the economy, represents a declining portion of the economy. Other sectors such as service, government, and non-profit have increased in relative importance, and they require greater prominence for management accounting. Second, there is in these sectors, a need for more detailed information at the level of the activities that comprise products and services. Third, information technology is now prevalent in the practice of management accounting. That information technology context needs to be incorporated into cases in order to make them more relevant. Accordingly, the book has three parts.

Section I describes management accounting case analysis. The second chapter explains the type of judgment that management accounting case analysis requires. Chapter 3 specifies those management accounting techniques which students will have opportunities to apply to their case analysis.

1

Chapter 4 contains a sample case that demonstrates the application of the case approach, and chapter 5 explains two approaches to case marking. A guided practice of case analysis is given in chapter 6. Chapter 7 introduces an approach to activity costing.

In Section II there are 26 cases for practice. Their contexts come from various industries, manufacturing, service, non-profit, and government. Taken together, they demand most of the management accounting techniques discussed in chapter 3.

This fourth edition introduces eight new cases that test students on contemporary management accounting techniques (balanced scorecard, cost of quality report, performance measurement, value chain) within emerging organizational contexts (best-in-class, business models, customer relationship management, enterprise resource planning systems, outsourcing, strategy, and total value creation).

Section III provides students with seven examples of activity costing in non-manufacturing organizations. Although the focus on activities is apparently new to academic management accounting, it has a long history in practice; for example, in industrial engineering and in productivity analysis.

REFERENCE

Kaplan, R.E., and H.T. Johnson, *Relevance Lost: The Rise and Fall of Management Accounting* (Boston, MA: Harvard Business School Press, 1987).

SECTION I

The Case Approach

CHAPTER 2

Developing Judgment

Case analysis is both teachable and learnable. It involves the use of judgment in complex practical situations, both in regard to the identification and analyses of issues, the choice of appropriate techniques, and recommendations for resolving the issues. Issues, analyses, and recommendations are the focus of this chapter. Techniques will be the focus of the next chapter.

EDUCATIONAL OBJECTIVES, AND WAYS OF THINKING

Understanding the educational objectives of the case approach will help students pursue these assignments effectively. The case objectives come from Bloom's taxonomy (Bloom et al., 1956), a taxonomy that accounting educators have accepted (Clevenger, 1990).

Bloom's educational objectives are:

1. **Knowledge**. This involves the recall of previously learned material. Students need to remember facts, principles, and steps in a sequence. A sample question that seeks out student knowledge would be, "define variable and fixed costs."

2. **Comprehension**. This involves the understanding of material presented in a course. At this level students explain, interpret, translate to a new form or symbol system, and extrapolate. A sample question would be, "explain an operating statement along the lines of variable costing."

3. **Application**. This involves the ability to use learning in other situations. Students are to use abstractions such as concepts, principles, rules, theories, and laws to find solutions to new problems. A sample question would be, "use contribution margin approach to explain the level of sales needed to break even."

4. **Analysis**. This is the capability for breaking course content into component parts in order to understand the relationships among parts. A sample question would be, "compare and contrast the operating statement for the company under absorption costing with direct costing."

5. **Synthesis**. This involves the putting together of parts to form a new whole. Students use what they have learned to produce new products such as themes, speeches, or research proposals. A sample question would be, from the evidence in the case, discuss how with an expansionary, high-end-of-the-market strategy the company became bankrupt.

6. **Evaluation**. This involves the ability to judge the value of material in light of a specific purpose using given criteria. Students make quantitative and qualitative judgments about the extent to which material and methods satisfy criteria. A sample question would be, "using the criteria of relevant and timely information for making decisions, evaluate the division's new information system compared to that which existed previously."

The case approach for management accounting presupposes that students possess a high degree of knowledge and comprehension, the first two of the six ascending educational objectives in the taxonomy. The primary focus of the case approach at this level is on application and analysis. Synthesis comes in, but to a lesser extent. More advanced courses would emphasize synthesis, and begin to develop competence in evaluation.

An example of a response that reveals application skills might be one in which the student considers the operating statements of an organization in comparison to the industry and realizes "the organization is performing more poorly than the industry average."

The student would exhibit analytical skill if they determined that:

- the contribution of all 12 sales regions;
- eight of the 12 sale regions were profitable and four were not;
- the unprofitable sales regions were in remote parts of the country, with higher turnover especially among managers who did not consider themselves truly part of the firm; and
- few managers of the unprofitable regions had promotions to corporate office jobs.

Synthesis builds upon application and analysis, and asks "what does it all mean?" Continuing with our example, a student could synthesize the evidence to explain that the poor profitability in the remote sales areas is a result of poor motivation, caused by the organization's neglect of the remote sales areas. As a consequence of this neglect, there is a higher than average turnover and the managers do not believe themselves to be integral parts of the company. Synthesis is the skill by which evidence is linked together, creating a plausible explanation.

DEFINITION OF A CASE QUESTION

Students need to begin with a clear understanding of the case method. Thompson and Strickland (1980) provide an insightful definition and explanation of a case, namely:

> A case sets forth, in a factual manner, the conditions and circumstances surrounding a particular managerial situation or series of events in an organization. It may include descriptions of the industry and its competitive conditions, the organization's background, its products and markets, the attitudes and personalities of the key people involved, production facilities, the work climate, the organization structure, marketing methods, and the external environment, together with whatever pertinent financial, production, accounting, sales, and market information upon which management has to depend. It may concern any kind of organization — profit-seeking business, or a public service institution.

The written description of the practical situation is called the case question. A good case question offers as real a practice situation as can be achieved short of the "real thing." It puts students at the scene of the action and familiarizes them with the actors and the contexts for their actions.

There are four objectives with the case method; awareness of these objectives will help students understand the process of case analysis. The first objective is to help the student learn to put management accounting techniques into practice. The second is to turn the student into an active learner rather than simply a passive accumulator of information. Case analysis helps students to acquire the habit of diagnosing issues, analysing and evaluating alternatives, and formulating workable plans of action. The third objective is to train students to work out answers for themselves, rather than relying upon the authority of the professor or a textbook. Finally, case analysis provides students with exposure to a range of organizations and management accounting situations, which otherwise would take a lifetime to experience personally. The exposure to a variety of situations will help students make career choices, as well as assist them in their careers.

RESPONDING TO A CASE QUESTION

This section will discuss the component parts of the case method and the student's responsibilities in completing an analysis. The focus of the section will be on helping the student to respond appropriately to a case question. As well, this section will provide some practical, "how to" advice. Based on the suggestions in this section, and with practice, students should be able to develop an approach to case analysis with which they are comfortable applying to various case questions.

There are two components to case analysis: the case question and the case response.

Case Question

The case question establishes the scenario or "story" of an organization. Typically, it includes characters — managers, workers, customers, etc., and a setting which will be some part or perspective of an organization. Cases can depict any type of organization, and there are many possible scenarios, given the number of management accounting topics and the equally large number of organizational types.

No matter what the scenario, there are issues or problems that must be resolved. An issue exists when there is a gap between expectations and actual performance in an area of an organization. For example, management accounting teaches students that organizations should have budgets for operational guidance. When a scenario states that an organization does not have a budget, then this is an issue.

The scenario of a case question will generally contain many issues concealed in comments made by case characters, findings by case characters, trends or ratios contained in financial statements, financial summaries, and industry comparisons. Identification of issues at first may be difficult. Through practice, however, students will become proficient at identifying as well as linking them.

One way to identify issues is to determine those attributes of the hypothetical organization that differ from the accounting and management practices which are taught as correct. Another method is to identify those attributes that lead to less than optimal economic performance. Examples include: declining sales in comparison to those of competitors, missed profit opportunities, managers insufficiently profit oriented, inaccurate budgeting, misleading cost accounting, ineffective sales incentives, and a failure to develop replacements for maturing products.

Imagine a case where two managers did not get along personally: A lumber manufacturing organization's log purchasing manager and mill manager refused to co-operate with each other. Their inability to co-operate led to a shortage of appropriate logs for a certain large and important order and caused other production scheduling problems as well. There are three issues in this example. First, personal conflict was affecting operations. Second, scheduling difficulties occurred. Third, management was unable to develop the necessary systems for scheduling that would work despite personal conflicts. For this example, the *root* issue was that "management was not able to develop the necessary systems." The other two issues, "personal conflict" and "scheduling deficiencies" are due to the lack of appropriate systems. With proper systems for scheduling that would work despite personal conflicts, "personal conflict" and "scheduling deficiencies" would not be problematic.

In addition to the scenario, the case question may contain a "required" which asks the student to do something. Typically, the required is the link between the case question and the case response. A required can be directed or non-directed, depending on the amount of direction provided to the student. Students should take special care to correctly understand the "required" before formulating the case response.

Learning to read a case efficiently and effectively is the key to good case analysis. Students should develop approaches that suit their typical reading strategies. Nevertheless, a recommended approach is to read the case quickly in order to get a sense of the context, and then to re-read it carefully and in detail. If one uses this approach, it is advisable to read the "required" before the second reading of the case. Re-reading with the "required" in mind allows one to discriminate between what is essential in the case and what is not.

Case Response

The case response is the student's answer to the case question. There is no one right or definitive answer to a case question. However, a student should not conclude that there are no wrong answers. Case responses differ because of differing identification of issues and analysis of relations among issues, differing determinations of what the root or underlying issues are, and differing development of recommendations to resolve the root issues and, in turn, the other issues. Although a variety of responses are valid at every stage, some, clearly, are incorrect.

The case response format is not fixed; typically it depends on the case question. However, using a simple, standardized form will improve case responses and provide a context for unambiguous marking. It is recommended that students use the issue-analyses-recommendations framework, deciding for themselves, according to the particular case, whether to use the three headings or to combine the first and second or the second and third. The three parts are described and analysed below.

Issues Problems or issues are those things that are wrong with the organization.

Students should read a case question once or twice to gather its essence. While reading, it is helpful to identify the issues by circling or highlighting them or by taking notes. Then, the student reviews these identified issues, adding to them any issues revealed by related analysis of financial statements and other supplementary information supplied.

In order to "size up" the root issues, it is essential to have a clear understanding of the organization and its issues. This analysis can be accomplished in two steps.

First, make a list of the issues. Arrange and assemble similar issues into groups. Explain the relationship among the groups or categories that emerge at this stage. The groupings should be governed by two criteria. First, same or related issues should be grouped together; for example, all issues related to inaccurate financial information would go into one group. Second, associations among issues within a group should be specified; for example, inaccurate accounting information led to poor decisions on inventory orders.

Second, the relationship among the categories must be explained. This explanation should reveal the real issues. Once they are disclosed, the real or root issues should be linked in a logical sequence. This listing should show the dependent relationship between the other issues and their root issues. Care should be taken to account for any specific requests that arise because of the role assigned to the student. For example, a case required that the student specify for the "president" the advantages of absorption costing over direct costing despite the apparent issues being unrelated to absorption and direct costing. Requests may be understood as additional issues.

The primary reason for grouping and ranking issues is to detect the underlying pattern of root issues. Sometimes, issues may also be the same as the root issues. In others, the detection may be more difficult. For example, consider a manufacturing firm with several problems; sales are not growing as expected, customers are returning products, customer satisfaction with the product quality is declining, and rework has increased. The root issue, lack of quality control, causes the other issues. Specifically, there was no quality control in the production process. The absence of quality control led to more rework and to the shipping of defective products, which the customers then returned or refused to buy again, and persuaded others not to buy.

It is identification of the root issues that enables the student to specify succinctly what is wrong with an organization. Proper identification requires close reading of the entire case, including appendices. Some information may have little or no bearing on the issues. As in the real-life situations that case analysis seeks to emulate, the student must sift carefully through all discernible aspects of a situation in order to determine which are relevant.

Analysis Analysis and issue identification are highly related. Analysis requires a thorough assessment of why an issue arose or exists, how various issues relate to each other, and which issues lead to others, and are therefore the most crucial to an understanding of the root issues. The analysis section includes required quantitative analysis; e.g., capital budgeting and variance analysis. The analysis discloses how well essential organizational functions are working; e.g., planning, controlling, and management information systems. Analysis can also reveal, when necessary, the strengths and weaknesses of the organization. The analysis may vary

in complexity. It can be as simple as listing the supporting issues, or as complex as finding the root or underlying issues.

Some case questions have a singular answer either because of the context or because of the "required." Other case questions lend themselves to a series of alternatives for solving issues. Alternatives should be individually meaningful and mutually exclusive. For example, for a business with serious profit problems, one alternative might be to reduce costs and focus on the core business. Another alternative might be to close the business and sell the assets and inventories. Each alternative must be explained and justified as an answer, and if appropriate, its advantages and disadvantages should be discussed.

Recommendations The recommendations are a student's approach to remedying the root issues. They should be selected from the alternatives discussed in the analysis section. In the course of resolving the root issues, the recommendations must also resolve most of the other issues. Recommendations should be action oriented, decisive and unambiguous; i.e., they should explicitly resolve the issues, assign responsibilities and set deadlines.

It may be suitable to include a conclusion that deals with implementation, especially with timing, and the assignment of responsibilities that arise out of the recommendations.

For the example, with respect to the organization with profit problems, a student might recommend cost cutting and focus on the core business alternative. The student should follow the selection of this alternative by specifying how it would resolve the profit problems, and by suggesting an implementation plan. The implementation should detail which costs are to be cut, by whom, and with what consequences. It should detail which businesses are to be eliminated, and which ones are to remain. If sufficient information is available, the recommendations should be quantified, showing the expected profit improvement.

In the report writing stage, it is often more time efficient and effective to identify, analyse, and make recommendations for each root issue individually. It is nevertheless essential to show the integration of the various issues within the case. Whatever the approach, it should be justified as the most appropriate for the case question.

TYPES OF CASES

Cases can be differentiated according to three characteristics: (1) the extent to which the "required" directs students, (2) the number of possible correct responses, and (3) the number of management accounting techniques evoked by the analysis. These characteristics are often interrelated.

The case's "required" can be direct or non-direct. A directed case leaves little opportunity for the student to decide the issues that need addressing; e.g., "calculate the net present value of a capital project." A non-directed case is just the opposite. Students must figure out the issues; e.g., "make recommendations to improve profitability."

The degree of directness of the "required" often relates to the number of possible correct responses. In non-directed cases, students can choose more than one way of seeing or grouping the issues, and so will arrive at a variety of appropriate sets of issues-analysis-recommendations. Consequently, there probably will be many correct responses, or solutions. At the other extreme, in a directed case, there are a restricted number of correct responses, possibly only one.

The number of management accounting techniques incorporated into a case can vary from as few as two to as many as 10 or 12. As a rule, the more techniques, the larger the number of possible acceptable responses, and the less directed the case.

This book consists largely of directed cases, each employing two or three management accounting techniques, and inviting several possible correct responses. This level of complexity is appropriate for intermediate management accounting students, and it is a step towards preparing students for minimally directed, multi-technique cases with many possible correct responses.

WRITING THE CASE RESPONSE

The role that the student is to play usually is established in the case question, sometimes in the "required." Also specified will be for whom the student is working. For example, the student may be a controller working closely with the president to determine funding for a capital project. As controller, the student must write a report to the president.

The case response in this context is prepared as a report. Typically it contains an introduction, and sections for issues, analysis, recommendations, and conclusion. The student should include a covering memorandum transmitting the report from the role played to the person or position for whom the work is being done. A short paragraph noting the report enclosed and linking it with the "required" is usually in order.

THE ROLE OF THE STUDENT

The essence of the student's role in case analysis is to diagnose and size up an organization's situation and to think through what, if anything, should be done. The student identifies and analyses the root and other issues, and proposes recommendations to resolve them. In formulating their analyses and recommendations, students must make assumptions about how the issues relate to one another. Their assumptions must be realistic, given the context of the question.

REFERENCES

Bloom, B.S., M.D. Englehart, G.J. Furst, W.H. Hill, and D.R. Krathwohl, *Taxonomy of Educational Objectives: The Classification of Educational Goals* (New York, NY: David McKay Co., 1956).

Clevenger, T.B., "The Cognitive domain of educational objectives: A model for future accounting education," presented to the American Accounting Association, 1990 annual meeting, Toronto, ON.

Thompson, A.A. Jr., and A.J. Strickland III, *Strategic Formulation and Implementation: Tasks of the General Manager* (Dallas, TX: Business Publications, 1980).

CHAPTER 3

Integrating Management Accounting Techniques

In their management accounting courses, students learn many techniques. They apply the techniques to problem-type questions where the requirements are explicit and where there are definite and usually singular answers.

Management accounting cases build upon this foundation of techniques, assuming students understand them. Cases test their judgment in selecting the most appropriate techniques for the issues. There will often be more than one approach or selection of techniques for resolving issues.

MANAGEMENT ACCOUNTING TECHNIQUES

The following is a list of management accounting techniques with which students should be familiar.

1. **Absorption costing**. This is a technique where the fixed costs as well as the variable costs are charged to the cost of goods or services produced.

2. **Activity-based costing**. A technique for allocating indirect costs with a two step procedure. The first is to accumulate the costs by functional activity. Then these costs are allocated to products or services with a denominator that is the activity that drives those functional costs.

3. **Allocation of costs**. The concept here is that of allocating or apportioning of costs to cost centres, products or services.

4. **Backflush costing**. A technique that attaches costs to outputs at the end of the period, without any costs attached to intermediate products during the period. Cost recording is simplified and its cost is reduced.

5. **Balanced scorecard.** A systematic performance measurement system that translates an organization's strategy into explicit objectives, mea-surements, targets, and initiatives organized by four perspectives; financial, customers, internal processes, and learning and growth.

6. **Budgets**. Using the framework of accounting reports, this is a technique that establishes expectations of what the transactions will be in some future period. As such it also establishes performance requirements and facilitates coordination among the different parts of an organization.

7. **Capital budgeting**. This is a budget for acquiring long-term assets. It quantifies benefits and costs of each major and distinct outlay, often called a project. Often the time value of money and risk are quantified. Techniques for evaluating the attractiveness of capital projects include net present value, internal rate of return, and payback.

8. **Contribution**. The difference between sales value and the variable costs of those sales, expressed either in absolute terms, as a percentage, or per unit.

9. **Control mechanisms**. They specify performance and/or then monitor results regarding planning and control decisions.

10. **Controllable cost**. The concept is applicable to where the responsibility centre manager can influence the cost.

11. **Cost behaviour**. The concept or idea that costs per unit of output are affected by fluctuation in the level of activity. Two techniques for analyzing cost behaviour are the high-low method and regression analysis.

12. **Cost-volume-profit analysis**. With the contribution as the denominator, this technique specifies the volume of sales needed to cover

predetermined fixed costs, income taxes, and profits.

13. **Decentralization**. This is the delegation of decision-making powers and responsibilities. Management accountants accept the concept that measurement systems need to accompany delegation for gauging the accomplishment of responsibilities.

14. **Flexible budgets**. The technique where variable costs are budgeted separately from fixed costs, and consequently the forecast of the projected level of costs given the volume and mix of activities undertaken.

15. **Incentives**. As a concept, management accountants accept that employees can be motivated to accomplish desirable results by making rewards contingent on the achievement of those results.

16. **Inventory management**. Management accountants use three techniques for managing inventory levels, i.e., economical order quantity, just-in-time, and materials requirements planning.

17. **Job cost**. A technique for costing goods or services, where the costs are added to each individually identified good or service, called a job.

18. **Joint costs**. The costs of providing two or more goods or services whose production cannot, for physical reasons, be segregated.

19. **Linear programming**. A technique for optimally allocating limited resources.

20. **Operation costing**. A cost allocation technique that is a hybrid between job and process costing. Each batch of products going through a process is considered a job.

21. **Outsourcing**. The process of buying resources from an outside supplier instead of producing them internally or in-house.

22. **Performance measurement**. The use of a numerical scale for the measurement of the performance of an operation or activity.

23. **Process costing**. A technique for allocating costs where the costs incurred for a period are averaged over all production units.

24. **Project control**. Projects are large jobs that extend beyond a single period. The technique of project control addresses completion time in addition to costs.

25. **Regression analysis**. As a technique for understanding cost behaviour, the coefficients in regression analysis are estimates of variable costs per unit costs — the slope — and the total fixed costs — the constant.

26. **Relevant costs, revenues**. These are the expected future costs or revenues that differ among alternative courses of action.

27. **Responsibility accounting**. This is the establishment of responsibility centres — cost, revenue, profit, or investment — under the responsibility of accountable managers.

28. **Standard costs**. To reduce recording time or costs, the technique of standard (or reliably estimated) costs is used instead of actual costs. Reconciliation occurs at the end of a period.

29. **Strategic control**. This is the concept of control at the aggregate level of an organization. Organizational objectives, missions, and strategies are examples, as they provide a context for detailed decisions and actions.

30. **Transfer price**. This is the price calculated for a good or service sold between related organizational units. It can be based on market, cost, and/or negotiation.

31. **Value chain.** The sequence of activities that make or deliver a good or service to customers. Each step in the chain should contribute more to the ultimate value of the product, in the eyes of the customer, than its cost.

32. **Variable or direct costing**. This is a technique where only the variable costs are charged to the cost of goods or services produced.

33. **Variance analysis**. This is the practice of comparing actual results to expectations established with budgets and/or standards. The differences are calculated, and may be explained and investigated, especially if the difference is significantly large and the benefit from the investigation is anticipated to exceed the cost.

CHAPTER 4

An Example and a Demonstration

The chapter presents a case and the steps of case analysis. The case in this chapter is qualitative; judgment is necessary to ascertain and assess the various issues. Cases can, of course, also be quantitative. Most cases in management accounting include a mix of qualitative and quantitative data. Read this case to see how a response is developed.

ONE-BIG-FIRM LTD.

The example case question shown on Exhibit 1 is typical of traditional management accounting cases. The handwritten notes in the margin and underlining are suggested techniques for identifying and analysing issues.

EXHIBIT 1: CASE QUESTION

Established in 1971, ONE-BIG-FIRM (ONE) has three operating divisions (Coszy House, Dishland, and Hammer and Nail) and a centralized purchasing and warehousing division. This arrangement led to profitable operations during the 1970s and 1980s. ONE expanded at a more rapid rate than could the three operating divisions if they were independent.

? Unusual organizational arrangement

During the 1990s, market conditions changed; retail expansion slowed. Many imitated ONE's volume approach, and some of these competitors have been doing better jobs at controlling costs. Market shares have declined, with the level of profitability falling for all three operating divisions.

— profit problems
— loss of customers

There are feelings throughout ONE that the product markets have matured, and that the future will not be pleasant for those who remain with the firm.

— morale (assumption)
— need new products or markets

Coszy House is a national volume retailer of upholstered and wooden household furniture. It has a strong market following and an 11 percent market share. Most of the furniture is purchased in the eastern part of the country and sold under the manufacturer's name. Inventory is purchased in advance and shipped to ONE's central warehouse. Later, the furniture is shipped directly to customers. Trucks move inventory both from the manufacturer to the central warehouse and from the central warehouse to the regional warehouses. The shipments to the regional warehouses are coordinated with periodic and planned sales events.

Why not ship direct?
— expensive
— high cost

Dishland is the division that sells a broad range of quality dishes and glassware. The products come from Great Britain and other European countries. Buyers from the Central Purchasing and Warehouse (CPW) division visit the manufacturers quarterly. The purchases are received at a major port, immediately shipped and initially stored in the central warehouse, and then shipped to the regional warehouses. After a customer orders, the merchandise comes from a regional warehouse. Later, the customer picks up the ordered merchandise. Sales are highly seasonal with 70 percent occurring during the last three months of each year. Except special promotions which account for 40 percent of annual sales, the demand is highly predictable. Moreover, there is little price or delivery time competition. Dishland is a large distributor in its field.

Hammer and Nail is a hardware chain with a product line that includes a full range of hardware supplies and equipment. With expansion, Hammer and Nail developed a high volume specialized warehouse facility in the central warehouse. Purchasing in volume and then repackaging into units sufficiently small for the stores led to substantial savings. This resulted in the division obtaining a 9 percent market share compared to 3 percent for the second largest competitor. The central warehouse stores hardware products before shipment to regional warehouses.

— strong competition

Why? ——
— bad
— unusual unresponsive to customers

The regional warehouses connect the stores through the central warehouse computer with direct order communication lines and, thus, orders can be quickly processed. In recent years, many hardware dealers have formed buyer cooperatives to exert pressure on manufacturers to provide lower prices. Also, manufacturers can provide smaller quantities per order through technological innovations.

The three operating divisions detail their monthly sales budgets one year in advance; CPW uses these budgets as a basis for planning its purchasing activities. CPW makes purchases to meet budgeted sales and to ensure adequate inventory in all regional warehouses for all three operating divisions. The rigidity of CPW's inventory requirements has benefited ONE through favourable prices on purchases to the extent of 2 percent on sales. Yet the fears of excess inventories and the difficulties in adjusting after the commencement of the fiscal year have encouraged CPW to purchase only those products that, based on past performance, are sure to sell. Operating divisions perceive this rigidity as the reason for losing opportunities to meet changes in market demand.

— serious problem

— finance is weak

There is a financial division responsible for all accounting, treasury, computer systems, and financial control activities. The finance division has never provided leadership. ONE places all other corporate functions under a vice-president of corporate services, e.g., personnel and labour relations, advertising, legal counsel, and insurance.

A basic policy of ONE is the charging out of non-operating or overhead costs. The operating divisions receive CPW costs based on sales volumes; these allocated costs have steadily increased from 6.3 percent five years ago to 12.7 percent. Comparable services cost about 3.5 percent of competitor sales. Non-operating divisions can pass on certain costs to the operating divisions with few restrictions. However, the operating divisions consider their actual performance to be before allocated costs.

— no incentive to minimize costs
— CPW is out of cost control

— bad

For the past seven years, the costs of CPW have increased at a more rapid rate than the costs and revenues of the operating divisions. The actual CPW costs have exceeded the budgeted costs in nearly each of those years. The operating divisions are unhappy with the responsiveness of CPW to their requirements. For the right product at the right price, CPW requires longer lead times than its more responsive competitors. To obtain greater responsiveness, two divisions have established expediting functions. All operating divisions have hired additional staff to help the coordination of activities with CPW. The coordinating employees duplicate some functions within the CPW division.

— CPW is out of cost control
— excess employees a symptom
— excess warehouse space

A recent study identified a need for only 75 percent of the warehouse space in the central warehouse. Of this required space, Coszy House uses two-thirds, while the other two divisions use the other one-third. Management has calculated similar utilization for the regional warehouses. Moreover, the president requested a national trucking firm to study ONE's transportation requirements. The trucking firm proposed for $5.2 million a year to move all merchandise from manufacturers to regional warehouses/ stores. This approach would lead to substantial savings. The back hauls, i.e., the trips that the trucks make back to the central warehouse, would no longer be empty. The president believes that competitive tendering would further reduce the present quoted price.

— investigate trucking offer

— excess costs
— tenders

Required

The president has asked you to identify methods for improving profitability. Prepare a report for the president including your findings, analysis, and recommendations.

Understanding the Case Question

The student is responsible for responding to the case's "required." In order to do so, the student must understand the case and its inherent issues. In order to identify the root issues, the student must start by identifying what appear to be the issues.

It is a helpful practice to gather the issues by reviewing one's case question margin notes and underlining. Case questions are always lean on detail, and thus, the student will always need to make reasonable assumptions for missing details. The following is a list of issues — the list is not exhaustive.

Profitability	Profitability has declined.
Competition	Competitors have replicated the successful market approach of the 1970s and 1980s, and often more cost effectively.
Responsiveness	The retail stores are not responsive to customers.
Budgeting	Budgeting is done far in advance, with little ability to adjust for changing market conditions.
Inefficiency	ONE is paying for trucks running empty on the back haul. Financial leadership is missing. Cost control is poor.
Warehousing and purchasing costs	These have grown faster than sales and other costs, and faster than competitors' expenses for the same outlays.
Staffing	To offset the poor service of CPW, the operating divisions hire extra employees.
Excess warehouse space	Current operating methods do not require 25 percent of the space.
Overhead	Operating divisions receive overhead costs on an actual cost basis, which provides no incentive for the overhead units to minimize costs.
Profit measurement	There is a lack of agreement on the measurement of operating profits.
Warehousing	Two levels of warehouses increase costs, with no additional improvement in service.
Trucking	Investigate the trucking offer as it is a means of reducing costs. Seek tenders.

ONE has some problems, which if left untended will lead to destruction. The overriding issue is that the current marketing strategy — central purchasing and warehousing — is no longer valid. Although the major issue is not directly stated, it is the theme that links many issues listed above. For example, the cost advantages of central purchasing and warehousing no longer offset the disadvantages of rigidity and unresponsiveness to demand, as the low profitability attests.

Other issues include the following:

- CPW is too expensive.
- There is unutilized warehouse space.
- There is surplus staff.
- There is no strategic plan.
- There is little concern for profitability.
- Financial leadership is missing.
- Morale is bad.

After arriving at an understanding of the major issue, and sketching out the analysis section, the next step is to write the case response. A case response example is given in Exhibit 2. It is just a possible response of many to the ONE case question's "required."

CONCLUDING COMMENTS

The case method replicates real life situations in a simplified way. It allows students to display their ability to apply what they have learned in management accounting courses. This chapter showed students how to write a case response without time constraints. In an examination setting, with time constraints, students may have difficulty identifying as many issues, and their analyses and recommendations may be more superficial.

EXHIBIT 2: CASE RESPONSE

(Memorandum)

TO: Ms. A.A. Smith, President

FROM: John Morris, Accountant

SUBJECT: Profitability Opportunities

Please find attached my report specifying the profit improvement opportunities you have requested. The report includes a discussion of the problems solved by the recommendations.

Sincerely,
John Morris

(Report)

Introduction

ONE-BIG-FIRM Ltd. (ONE), a diversified retail firm with activities across Canada, has three operating divisions and centralized purchasing and warehousing. Senior managers are concerned with the level of profitability. The president requested the report for identifying profit opportunities.

Issue Identification

As requested, I reviewed ONE's operations. I analysed many issues for common threads and causal relationships. Eight major or root issues emerged:

- The current marketing strategy — central purchasing and warehousing — is no longer valid.
- CPW is too expensive.
- There is unutilized warehouse space.
- There are surplus employees.
- There is no strategic plan.
- There is little concern for profitability.
- Financial leadership is missing.
- Morale is bad.

Analysis and Recommendations

1. **The marketing strategy is inappropriate**.

   The marketing strategy is obsolete. Although the central purchasing and warehousing approach worked well in the 1970s and 1980s, competitors have imitated ONE, and controlled costs. Rather than being an advantage, central purchasing and warehousing is now more expensive than alternative approaches employed by competitors. Moreover, the current marketing approach is rigid and non-responsive to the needs of customers.

   Recommendations: Develop a strategy for getting ONE out of the current strategic problem. This will involve primarily a marketing strategy that stresses customer responsiveness and market share.

2. **CPW is too expensive**.

   Central purchasing and warehousing cost 12.7 percent of sales compared to 3.5 percent for equivalent services with competitors. There is a 2 percent advantage on purchases with central purchasing. The total disadvantage is 7.2 percent of sales.

   Recommendations: Decentralize the purchasing and warehousing operations. This will mean dismantling CPW, and restructuring those functions to something comparable to the competitors of the operating divisions. The result, reduced costs to competitor levels, will add to profits.

EXHIBIT 2...cont'd

3. **There is underused warehouse space.**

   Lease the 25 percent vacant space. Warehouse requirements could further decline if vendors ship directly to regional warehouses or retail stores.

   Recommendations: Sub-lease excess warehouse space. With the decentralization of purchasing and warehousing there will be even less need for the warehouses. The most profitable option may be to sell the central warehouse and require vendors to ship to regional warehouses or to retail stores.

4. **There are surplus employees.**

   Because of the poor service by the central purchasing and warehousing division, the operating divisions have hired expediting staff. If CPW was responsive to the operating divisions, the expediters would not be needed.

   Recommendations: Redeploy expediting employees and reduce costs.

5. **There is no strategic plan.**

   ONE has been blindly pursuing one strategy without the preparation for eventual modification or replacement of that strategy — central purchasing and warehousing — when it lost its viability.

   Recommendations: Develop a strategic plan to prepare for the future.

6. **There is little concern for profitability.**

   ONE has seen its level of profitability decline significantly in recent years, but it has not proposed serious remedies. In addition, cost control has never been seriously considered, as shown by the allocation of actual overhead costs to the operating divisions.

   Recommendations: Profitability should be given more importance. Develop a financial orientation. Establish financial goals with budgets and plans. Use incentives to obtain higher profitability.

7. **Financial leadership is missing.**

   Many serious financial deficiencies exist. There is controversy over the measurement of operating income. The system for allocating overhead costs to the operating divisions (i.e., based on actual costs and sales) does not provide an incentive to minimize costs. Actual CPW costs have exceeded budget.

   Recommendations: Appoint a dominant vice-president, finance and support him/her. Develop operating statements that measure what managers have control over and hold them accountable for achieving budgets.

8. **Morale is bad.**

   The decline in profitability and the relative improvement of competitors have led staff to believe there to be a poor future for ONE and its employees.

   Recommendations: Discuss planned changes with employees, and the benefits that will accrue. Allow staff to participate in planning.

Other Issues

The trucking offer should be considered. This offer is based on having other freight on the back haul and thus not returning at cost to ONE. To ensure the best deal, ONE should go to tender. Regardless of who wins the contract, this route is preferable to the present situation of paying for empty trucks on the back haul. Sell the existing trucks and re-deploy the affected staff.

Conclusion

It is crucial for ONE to proceed immediately with the recommendations. The President should be responsible for their implementation because of their significance to the firm's viability.

CHAPTER 5

Marking Cases

Understanding how cases are marked clarifies the expectations underlying case analysis, and so it can be helpful.

There are two basic approaches to marking cases: mechanical and global. Mechanical or analytical marking involves identifying all possible aspects of a perfect answer and assigning a point value to each. This is a thorough, detailed, and time-consuming approach to case marking. The other method is called global (rating or holistic) marking which takes less time and is less detailed. Global marking involves identifying all important issues. Each response is judged as to how these major issues are addressed. With global marking each paper is generally marked twice. Significant differences between marks must be resolved. The advantage of global marking over mechanical marking is that it is not biased against short, uniquely insightful case responses. The lack of detail is its disadvantage.

Each method is discussed with an example.

MECHANICAL MARKING

As there is no singularly correct answer, mechanical marking must allow for all reasonable perceptions of the issues. To give credence to the expectation of more than one appropriate response, mechanical marking guides must have more marks than the total for the case question. For example, if there are 70 marks for a case question like ONE-BIG FIRM Ltd. in chapter 4, the marking guide could have 139 marks as noted in this chapter. Seldom do students earn the full marks allotted because of limited time, and because some marks overlap with each other. Thus, any response justified with evidence in the case question will receive marks..

There is another way to explain excess marks. Case questions contain issues or evidence on fundamental or root issues. However, the linkage between an issue and a root issue is not explicit. Students must argue the relationship. For example,

in the case response in chapter 4, the root issue is "current marketing strategy is inappropriate." This is not in the case question, but evidence in the case supports it, e.g., the once successful central purchasing and warehousing approach is more expensive than what competitors use.

Exhibit 3 displays a mechanical marking guide which contains examples of individual preferences for conceptualizing the root issues. Two of the root issues — number 1 "marketing strategy inappropriate" and number 5 "no strategic plan" — relate to long term, major decisions on how to carry out the business of ONE. The marking guide includes both to reward the various "right answers."

Whenever students mention issues and root issues, they get rewarded with marks. Their issues and root issues may not line up as shown above. Nevertheless, the mechanical markers seek to reward marks against the most appropriate categories on the guide, and sometimes generously.

Besides issues, analysis, and recommendations, there are marks for format and professionalism. Such rewards should be kept in mind when writing the case response, as a little time may pay handsomely. For example, precede the case response with a memorandum. This should be from the person that the student is role playing, to the person and position to whom the case suggests the student is to report. The memorandum should contain a short paragraph linking the case question required with the attached report. The report itself should have headings, e.g., introduction, issues, analysis, recommendations, and conclusion. When using point form, introduce it with a sentence. There should a logical flow to the report. And there should be no glaring deficiencies with grammar, spelling, and sentence structure.

GLOBAL MARKING

This method of marking starts with a ranking of the most important issues that need to be addressed. Then, each issue receives a point score

EXHIBIT 3: MECHANICAL MARKING GUIDE

			Marks	Sub-total
1.	**Issue**	marketing strategy inappropriate	3	
	Analysis	obsolete	2	
		competition	2	
		too expensive	2	
		rigid, non-responsive	2	
	Recommendation	develop new marketing strategy	2	13
2.	**Issue**	CPW too expensive	3	
	Analysis	costs, 12.7%	2	
		competition, 3.5%	2	
		2% advantage on purchases	2	
		7.2% total disadvantage	2	
	Recommendation	decentralize purchasing	2	
		dismantle CPW	2	
		reduce costs	2	17
3.	**Issue**	underutilized warehouse space	3	
	Analysis	25% vacant	2	
		could ship directly	2	
	Recommendation	sublease	2	
		sell	2	11
4.	**Issue**	surplus staff	3	
	Analysis	poor service from CPW	2	
		additional staff required	2	
		CPW should be responsive	2	
	Recommendation	redeploy expediting staff	2	
		reduce costs	2	13
5.	**Issue**	no strategic plan	3	
	Analysis	blind pursuit of obsolete strategy	2	
		no preparation for changes	2	
	Recommendation	develop a strategic plan	2	9
6.	**Issue**	little concern for profitability	3	
	Analysis	profits have declined significantly	2	
		unabated	2	
		cost control missed	2	
		cost allocation dispute	2	
	Recommendation	profitability to be emphasized	2	
		develop financial orientation	2	
		develop financial goals	2	
		use financial incentives	2	19
7.	**Issue**	financial leadership missing	3	
	Analysis	income measurement controversy	2	
		actual costs rather than standard	2	
		cost minimizing incentives missing	2	
		CPW costs have exceeded budget	2	
	Recommendation	appoint a dominant v-p finance	2	
		develop financial measures	2	15
8.	**Issue**	morale is bad	2	
	Analysis	problems have depressed employees	2	
	Recommendation	discuss turn-around	2	
		allow employee participation	2	8
9.	**Other issues**	trucking offer — consider	2	
		back haul	2	
		tender	2	
		sell trucks	2	
		redeploy employees	2	
		other	10	20
*	**Format**	focus on profit improvement	2	
		logical in sequence	2	
		supported statements and assumptions	2	
		spelling and grammar	4	
		addressed to the president	2	
		general impression	2	14
				139

Student mark /70 (Maximum)

```
┌─────────────────────────────────────────┐
│                                           │
│      EXHIBIT 4: MARKING GUIDE — GLOBAL    │
│                                           │
│   Issues                                  │
│      1.  New strategy needed        25    │
│      2.  Costs out of control       20    │
│      3.  Financial leadership needed 10   │
│                                           │
│   Focus                                   │
│      4.  Sense of urgency, understanding 10│
│      5.  Professionalism             5    │
│                                     ───   │
│                                     70    │
│                                           │
└─────────────────────────────────────────┘
```

consistent with the ranking. For each issue, a single student score would be awarded based on the identification of the issue and related issues, analysis, and recommendations for resolution. Other factors such as professionalism and realism can be scored also.

Global marking places more emphasis on the subjective judgement of the marker. It usually takes a few dozen papers before marking consistency can be established. The use of two markers is recommended to reduce bias. This can be waved in favour of time savings when the marker has substantial experience with the case or the case is uncomplicated.

For the example of ONE, the marking guide for global marking could look like the one shown on Exhibit 4.

CASE WRITING TACTICS

The method of marking should not affect how a student responds to a case question. Mechanical marking might favour students using a "shotgun" approach of putting every possible thing down on the case response. Such an approach usually leads to duplication and not much depth or linkage among the various facets of a case question. It would be a poor examination tactic, as it takes time away from a thorough and systematic approach to the case question. Given the time constraints, students should seek to manage their time by understanding the root issues vis-à-vis the

required. They should emphasize identifying, analysing, and resolving those root issues, and, only when time is available, discuss the more tangential issues.

Global marking might favour short, uniquely insightful responses. A well-designed mechanical marking guide should do the same. Seeking short, uniquely insightful responses could be dangerous as such responses usually take substantial sifting through the data to find one that addresses all issues or at least all root issues. It usually takes less time to address issues individually than in total.

A case response that will yield a passing mark must show depth of analysis. This requires sufficient time spent reading the case question in order to understand the case and its issues. The student then has the evidence pointing to the root issues, and can undertake the analysis, and to make appropriate recommendations. If insufficient time is spent reading, the student will have a superficial response and be unable to say much about the issues or to recommend solutions. In a timed situation, however, spending too much time reading leaves insufficient time for responding. Consequently, students should set in advance the length of their reading time and stick to it. To be able to do this, a student needs to understand a variety of possible cases, and have a rule for each type. Students should develop their rules that satisfy their own approaches. Two extreme examples follow.

1. For multi-technique cases like ONE, 40 percent of the time could be spent reading and 60 percent spent writing. While reading, the relationships between issues and root issues, analysis, and recommendations emerge. Writing time includes time to refine understanding. More ideas will emerge during the writing stage.

2. For a quantitative, directed case like Precious Metals — case 21 of this selection — the reading time might fall to about 15 percent or even less, as the real issues are blatant.

For the majority of student case responses, the earned marks will be the same under both mechanical and global marking.

CHAPTER 6

A Practice Case

Case analysis is the application of management accounting techniques to practical issues and/or real-life situations. In simple cases, the appropriate techniques and issues are explicit. In more complex cases, the appropriate techniques and issues are harder to ascertain.

This chapter and the casebook seek to develop student skills in doing case analysis. The underlying premise is that instruction, coupled with practice and feedback, will produce understanding of the case approach. A first step is provided by this chapter. It explicitly specifies in advance a management accounting technique to be applied to a case question. Normally, the student must determine the management accounting technique. However, by specifying the technique, this chapter explains how

case questions are viewed from the perspective of a particular management accounting technique in determining issues.

Management Accounting Technique

For the case in this chapter, the management accounting technique will be "feedback information." This technique incorporates the belief that information on operations and employee behaviour will facilitate improvements to future performance. This is an underlying belief with financial and non-financial reports.

The case displayed in Exhibit 5, Computer Sales Division, is to be read and during the reading, it is to be assessed from the perspective of feedback information. This technique implies

---

EXHIBIT 5: COMPUTER SALES DIVISION

You were a commissioned sales representative for five years. Although business was competitive, for three of those years, you were the top sales representative for your company.

You thoroughly enjoyed your job. You had substantial independence. You selected the firms you wanted to contact. You determined the sales approach. There were no inhibiting rules or regulations. Your boss did not interfere, but instead bought you lunch every first Monday of the month. You did what you wanted to do because you were the top sales representative.

Fourteen months ago your boss retired and you received his position as the sales manager, central division. Your subordinates include 24 commissioned sales persons, two order processing clerks, and a secretary/receptionist.

On the first day of your new job you made two commitments. First, you told your new boss, the vice president of sales, that your unit's sales and profits would increase by 20 percent in the next year. Second, you gave the sales staff of your unit five steps that if followed would double their sales.

Now you regret those commitments. The first year has transpired. Sales are down 15 percent. Profits are down 25 percent. And rather than doubled, sales per sales person are down 10 percent and three sales representatives have gone with a competitor.

In reflecting over the last year, your comments to the sales representatives keep coming back.

The rules for successful selling are simple. By following my five rules, your personal sales will double and with our commission structure so will your gross income. The rules are:

1. Call all regular customers at least once every two weeks. Ask if they are planning to buy computers, equipment, or software. Emphasize that you would be pleased to provide quotations.

2. New customers are essential for sales growth. Make 25 cold calls each month. Five should become new customers. I get company names from the yellow pages, trade directories, etc. With cold calls, I use the telephone and ask the answering receptionist for the person in charge of computer purchases. This usually leads to a few calls and questions before I reach the person most likely to be able to make purchases from us. I present myself, our company, and the fact that we supply and support IBM compatible equipment and software.

3. I meet my active clients regularly. Clients with sales potential of less than $150,000 are met once a year. See clients twice a year if they have more potential.

4. Every month I send each active client something in the mail or through E-mail that keeps them aware of my name and telephone number.

5. I return all calls within an hour. This requires an answering service (no voice mail), a cellular telephone, and a beeper.

   With these steps I can work independently and effectively. I meet only once every month for lunch with my boss and all he did was to keep me informed about our new products.

These five steps have come to haunt you. All sales representatives have adamantly said they followed the five steps. They blame you for their failures. You do not know if they are telling the truth, or if they are not following the steps, or if the procedures are not effective for all sales representatives.

Very concerned with the decline in sales, the vice president reviewed the five steps and admitted their validity. However, he suggested that they may not represent all the steps for successful selling. As an example, he mentioned that the content of discussions with clients and methods for closing a sale are important, but not included in the five steps. He also informed you that there have been complaints about sales representatives who compete with one another for the same orders.

You are confused. You know how to sell but you do not know if your sales representatives know how.

Required

Using the case approach and the feedback information perspective, identify the root issues, analyse them, and make recommendations for resolving the issues.

that feedback is useful and necessary if management is to be successful in directing employees. Consequently, the lack of feedback means that management is less than optimal and that problems have or will occur because of the lack of feedback.

CHAPTER 7

Analysing Activities

A current trend in management accounting textbooks is to focus on activities. The activities that form costs are the concern, not resultant dollars per se. Managers need to manage activities to influence product and service costs.

The management of activities has long been associated with scientific management and Frederick Taylor (1911), an early and vocal proponent. More recently, Michael Porter (1980, 1985) has supported the activity focus. He argues that the value of a product or service in the eyes of consumers is a result of activities. Keep the activities that add value, discard the others.

This chapter of the book encourages students to venture into non-manufacturing organizations — service, trade, government, and nonprofit—to study and apply management accounting at the activity level. A general framework provides assistance to the venture. Real organizations are to be chosen, but students are not to select an entire organization. They should examine some meaningful but distinct part. Ideally there will be seven to twelve employees with three or four different position classifications. The requirement is for depth of analysis and not broad and superficial coverage.

Students are to work together in groups of two to four and they must prepare a proposal. The proposal, about one page, should identify the organization, unit, number of employees and positions, and discuss the project steps. Approval of the proposal by the instructor is mandatory. Results of the project are to be written up in a formal report with introduction and conclusion — a recommended length of 12 to 15 pages, plus appendices. The following list contains the steps:

1. **Describe the organization and unit**. This section should be brief, but emphasis should be placed on what is important to the organization and how the unit contributes to the achievement of organizational objectives.

2. **List all activities**. In fulfilling the requirements of a position an employee undertakes many activities. Students are to aggregate the activities of each classification into a few activities, probably four to eight significant ones. Describe the relationship between activities and positions with flow diagrams. (This technique is described in Exhibit 6.) Use a matrix to show the activities associated with each position. The matrix will simplify scheduling and suggest where cross training will increase flexibility in scheduling the accomplishment of the unit's responsibilities.

The emphasis should be on actual activities that drive costs — such as taking an order, processing an invoice and changing four tires — and not responsibilities. For some, especially senior positions, activities will be difficult to document. A block of time may be the best means of assigning time, e.g., a supervisor's time for recruitment.

3. **Conduct observations**. Students are to observe and time employees undertaking activities. Through these observations, establish work-to-time relationships, i.e., figure out the time required to complete each activity. This will tend to be an average time and there will be a variance around the average.

4. **Identify activity changes**. From observations or analysis, students are to develop better methods for performing some activities, i.e., reduce costs, increase value. Students should consider changes to work flow, work methods, procedures, etc. that will allow activities to be streamlined and done in less time.

5. **Establish standards**. Based on observations and in consultation with the unit's manager and employees, choose reasonable time standards for performing each activity. Incorporate the required level of service or quality in the standard. A standard is not necessarily an average. It is a reasonable goal for a good employee working at a reasonable rate.

6. **Gather activity driver data**. To assign employees to work, it is first necessary to gather historical data on activity drivers, by time of year, week, or day, etc. An activity driver is an event associated with the activity that results in the consumption of the organization's resources. For example, Mexican FFF has a dominant activity driver in the number of orders. With more orders, crew members have more activities for serving customers, preparing food, and delivering food. Some activities are without activity drivers. Assign blocks of time for those activities, e.g., allocate one hour a day to the manager for scheduling employees at Mexican FFF. If actual data are not available, consult the unit's manager and employees for estimates. These data should result in workable, simple, and meaningful activity driver models showing differences during the year, week, or day. Remember, it is the activity driver that leads to the need for activities.

7. **Determine employee hour requirements**. Using the above models for activity drivers and the established standards, calculate the number of employee hours to accomplish the requisite activities individually and in total. A simplified example would be where the activity driver is the number of customers, and where the model specifies 150 clients a day. With, say 10 activities to serve a client totalling 16 minutes, the need is for 2,400 minutes (150 × 16) or 40 hours of employee time. Typically, models would be more complicated and the employee hour requirements differ by time of year, week, or day.

8. **Schedule employees**. Make suggestions for the scheduling of employees for effectively and efficiently accomplishing the unit's activities while adding value. Recognize that employees cannot work at 100 percent utilization. Employees frequently and legally have work (i.e., coffee) breaks. Moreover, employees

---

EXHIBIT 6: STRUCTURED SYSTEMS ANALYSIS

This flow diagramming technique describes business activities for formulating computer applications. It is also effective in business improvement studies. Structured systems analysis (SSA) works on the idea that a picture (or a diagram) is worth a multitude of words. The inherent clarity of a diagram is not easily replicated in words alone.

For the management accountant, SSA has two advantages. First, it enhances the understanding of the activities within an organizational unit. It concentrates on detailed activities. These activities comprise the basis of responsibilities for aggregate revenues and costs. This allows questioning of what is being done (e.g., is an activity really necessary), how the activity is being done (e.g., are there means for increasing efficiency and/or effectiveness), and what is a reasonable time for accomplishing an activity? This enhanced understanding allows management accountants to better identify opportunities for improvement. The second advantage is that SSA allows the management accountant to develop or assist in the development of an information system based on insightful and controllable activities.

There are only five symbols for diagramming with SSA. SSA's graphic language provides a versatile vehicle for understanding an organizational unit at the activity and sub-activity level. The symbols are described below. The example on page 24 illustrates an application of the symbols to an organizational unit from a provincial social services department.

Symbols

Activities:
- Process identification
- Descriptive name
- Position performing activity

External Entities:
- Source or destination for activities/data, i.e., anything outside the particular set of activities
- Duplication symbol

Storage of data regarding activities

Data or information flow

Activity flow

References

Mendes, K.S., "Structured systems analysis: a technique to define business requirements," Sloan Management Review, Summer 1980, pp. 51–63.

Ozerkevich, M.J., and G.P. Spraakman, "Adding rigor to management: A case study of structured systems analysis," Optimum, 1987, No. 2, pp. 22–37.

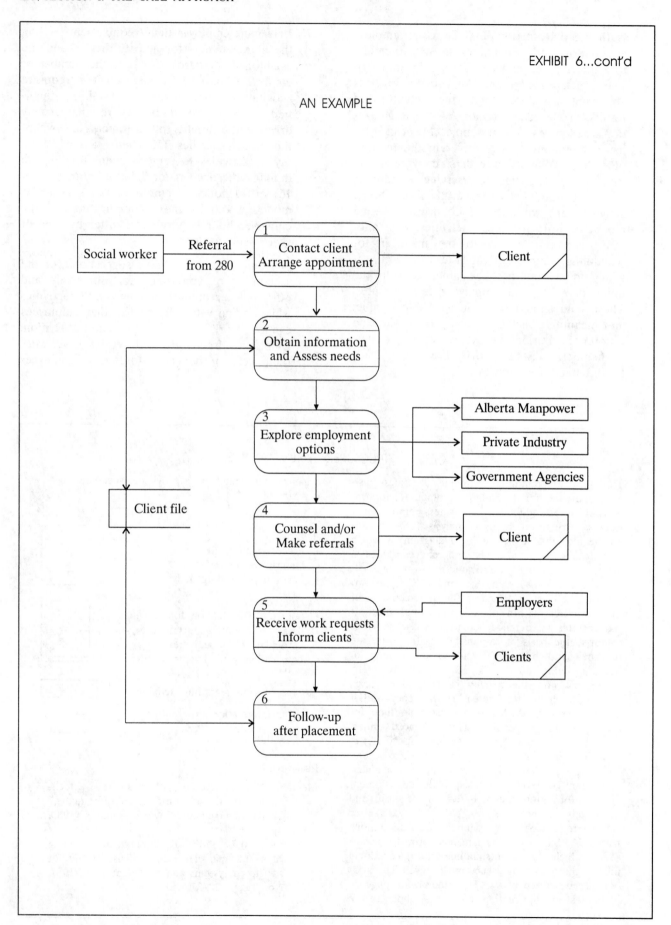

AN EXAMPLE

make personal telephone calls and engage in social (non-organizational) talk, without threat or loss of their jobs. Thus, employees do not work 100 percent of the time, but 85 percent or 90 percent of the time after deducting coffee breaks. The important goal is the accomplishment of a unit's required activities, while maintaining the target utilization rate. Employee hour requirements suggest part-time employees for peak activity levels instead of full-time employees who would be under-used during slow activity periods.

9. **Develop an information system**. With the understanding of how activities get accomplished, develop a feedforward and feedback system for managing employees. This should start with activity drivers expectations for a year, week, or day. Then schedule the number of employees needed to meet this volume of activity drivers. The standard time per activity and the utilization rate directly influence the number of employees required. An information system would compare these expectations with the actual activity driver volumes, scheduled employees, and utilization rates. It would suggest the appropriateness of the standards. In many ways this would be a flexible budget, complete with actual results and variance analysis, but at the level of activities instead of dollars. This system should be simple and explicit. It should add value in the eyes of the customer.

There are seven cases in Section III for applying activity costing to service organizations. Three cases display complete applications of the project approach outlined in this chapter. Four cases provide the contexts to which students are to apply the project steps from "identifying activity changes" to "scheduling employees."

REFERENCES

Porter, M.E., *Competitive Strategy* (New York, NY: Free Press, 1980).

———, *Competitive Advantage* (New York, NY: Free Press, 1985).

Taylor, F.W., *The Principles of Scientific Management* (New York, NY: Harper & Brothers, 1911).

SECTION II

Management Accounting Cases

Atcom Manufacturing

Atcom is an international firm that specializes in the manufacture of telecommunication equipment. It was the manufacturing subsidiary and major supplier to a provincial telephone utility. With its early success, Atcom started to sell to customers other than its parent. Then, as part of a privatization policy, the provincial government issued 40 percent of Atcom's common shares to the citizens of the province.

Subsequently, Atcom expanded to a national and more recently an international (with one plant in the United States) sales and manufacturing organization. Two years ago, under pressure from customers and potential customers, the parent sold all but 10 percent of its shares. That divestment became part of a strategic plan which emphasized an increased level of new product introduction, especially in respect to computer and electronic technologies.

Within the last year, this accelerated introduction of new products has led to problems with the firm's standard cost system. To explain these problems, it is necessary to understand the various controls that are in place at Atcom. Atcom adopted its parent's control system, with few changes. Thus, Atcom updates its long-range (10-year) plan every two years. Quarterly updates supplement the annual budget and monthly reports against the original budget. Plans and budgets emphasize accountability, and they are done at all levels designated as profit, revenue, or cost centres. The MIS department prepares reports on non-financial information, e.g., capacity utilization, product quality, customer satisfaction. Sales forecasts are the basis of the budgets, and standards are the basis for production costs.

With this overlay of planning, budgeting, and management information systems, every unit of the organization is subject to standard operating activities, an inheritance from the utility parent. Documented activities specify exactly how employees are to undertake their responsibilities. With each unit an experienced staff (which reports to the president) develops the standards. The detailed operating activities specify the steps that employees must perform, parts, materials, etc. In this way, operating activities provide the basis for evaluating employee performance.

The problem with the standard costs is a result of the rapid rate of new product introduction. The eventually established operating activities are often different and inconsistent with costs committed for new products. Consequently, standard costs may be impossible to meet or they could be insufficiently demanding. Employees are uncertain about the reasonableness of committed costs, and often there is a lack of motivation to achieve perceived unfair standards.

The president hired you to provide advice on how to resolve the standard cost problem and to get commitment to the budgets and timetable for new products. Within the first few days, you realize that there are two opinions. Among the manufacturing employees, particularly the supervisors, the consensus is that they want to develop detailed activities (i.e., standard operating procedures) before committing to standard costs. They recognize and welcome the expectation that there will be a learning curve and lower unit costs as production volumes increase. However, they insist upon a factual starting point consisting of activities by the accountable employees.

The other consensus comes from the marketing people. They say the standards cannot wait for the detailed activities behind the standard costs. They admit to the thoroughness and reduced risk from activities-based standard costs. They insist, however, that taking the time to establish the detailed activities will delay the introduction schedule for each new product by between six months and one year, and that delay has already caused problems for them. To resolve the conflict they suggest that standard costs should be expected results, from which several different sets of activities could then be selected. Some marketing people are even questioning the need for standard costs.

They cite as evidence in favour of eliminating standard costs, just-in-time inventory systems, the large proportion of purchased components, and the declining share of costs going to direct labour.

Required The president has asked you to implement a solution for introducing new products without delay or lack of control.

Bert the Baker

You are a management accountant with the divisional accounting office of a large grocery retailer, Foodco. Your supervisor has asked you to go to the Richville store to resolve an issue the store manager has with the bakery manager about the fairness of the accounting information used with a bonus system.

In order to remain viable and to grow, Foodco introduced sales and profit targets for retail stores. For an "A-type" store like the Richville store, the weekly sales target is $12 per square foot, or for this 20,000 square-foot store, $12.5 million a year. Operating profits are to be 5 percent of target sales, or $625,000 a year.

Typically, store managers delegate responsibility for sales and operating profits to department managers, i.e., produce, dry goods, bakery, and meats. With this system, the store managers and their department managers receive bonuses equal to about one-third of their salaries if the targets are both achieved.

Upon arriving at the Richville store, you meet Stella, the store manager, and then Bert, the baker. Bert reiterates his complaint that the bonus system is based on unfair accounting.

I am told that my sales target is $1.75 million a year or about $33,655 a week. I have no problem with sales. I can provide customers with what they want at competitive prices. However, I have a problem with my annual profit target of $150,000 which is 8.5 percent of sales. My complaint has nothing to do with the 8.5 percent profit target being more than the 5 percent for the overall store. A bakery has a better chance of high profits than the other departments.

Let me explain. First, I have little control over my labour costs. The store manager schedules employees who may or may not be necessary for the bakery. Second, the bakery operating statement includes charges that have nothing to do with the bakery. For example, the store manager's total salary is charged to the bakery because it is always profitable. Third, I do not get the chance to approve any of the costs charged to the bakery department. Fourth, I do not receive a copy of the bakery operating statement. Fifth, and most important, there is no opportunity to plan the operating costs in conjunction with the store manager and the other department managers. This would allow costs to be managed more carefully.

Required As the management accountant, you are to use the case approach to identify and analyze the issues and make recommendations for their resolution.

Brights Lodging and Travel

Some owners of hotel properties have been establishing new medium-priced, good quality hotels in dilapidated downtown locations. The new properties are either new buildings built on vacant land or major renovations to existing buildings, previously used for other purposes. There are two reasons for placing new hotels into seedy downtown areas where the neighbours might include ramshackle rows of shops, nightclubs with bullet-proof glass, and homeless people. First, there is the strategy of developing up-and-coming locations in major U.S. cities, and thereby taking advantage of the expected return of people to inner cities. These properties are a bet on urban renewals and increased property values. Second, these downtown hotels provide convenient accommodations for busy business travellers who want good quality without paying for unnecessary opulence. They are also a wager on a change in business practices from opulence to basic quality saving travellers money and increasing the returns to hotels.

There is a simple but consistent format for each hotel chain participating in these urban renewals. For one major chain the rooms surround a central pool, there is plenty of parking for rental cars, all rooms have functional desks and data ports for laptops, and the modest lobbies have breakfast buffets. Their uniformity makes these urban renewals easy to spot, and thereby reduces the need for advertisement.

A new building on vacant land does not pose any significant problems. Renovating existing alternative use buildings can have problems, and these renovations may be 20 to 30 percent more expensive than comparable new buildings. Renovations may be further complicated. Antiquated plumbing and electrical systems often are more expensive to rebuild than to replace with new systems. Older buildings have layouts that pose challenges. One renovation example is where two king-size beds fit in room 801 but not into 701. The problem is that the building's walls are inches thicker at the base, making the lower-floor rooms smaller. Nevertheless, renovations are often required to meet specific municipal regulations.

During the past year, Brights Lodging and Travel Corporation (BLT) has managed 26 of these urban renewal hotels, and it has signed an agreement to manage another six for another hotel chain starting next year. It should be noted that there are often two players in the delivery of hotel services. First, there are the owners of the hotel buildings, such as those developing no-frills urban renewals. Second, there are the management companies such as BLT who manage the hotels. The latter hire all employees, buy all supplies and food, and maintain all equipment and facilities. These management firms work on the basis of a share of the top-line revenue or a share in the profits. BLT is an example of a hotel management company.

As the management accountant at BLT you have been asked by the board of directors and the CEO (who is a member of the board and a major shareholder of BLT) to develop a balanced scorecard. She recently attended a hotel management conference where there was a session on the benefits from using the balanced scorecard. To advise you, the CEO has formed a committee consisting of herself, the controller, two owner representatives, and three general managers from successful BLT-managed hotels.

The committee established a series of meetings to exchange information for guiding you with the balanced scorecard. In the end, they provided you with advice on all four perspectives of the balanced scorecard.

Financial Perspective

The committee noted that financial measures have been the basis for gauging the effectiveness of hotel management despite other factors such as customer satisfaction and employee (associate) turnover having a direct affect on financial performance. BLT uses ACCPAC to produce operating statements for each hotel and chain with the for-

EXHIBIT 1: OPERATING STATEMENT

	Latest Year
Rooms available	108,405
Rooms occupied	86,714
Average rate	82.79
Revenue	
Rooms	$7,179,052
Food	306,198
Beverage	51,203
Telephone	289,890
Other	138,468
Total	7,964,811
Cost of goods sold	
Telephone	42,257
Telephone equipment	22,893
Other	311,001
Total cost of goods	376,151
Payroll	
Housekeeping	466,472
Laundry	53,987
Front desk	122,550
Administration	86,123
Sales	27,024
Maintenance	82,286
Management (salary)	279,335
Employee relations	25,670
Other	121,455
Total payroll	1,264,902
Controllable expenses	
Linen and laundry	46,826
Guest supplies	70,983
Cleaning expense	44,867
Rooms, other	92,022
Postage	9,750
Office supplies	20,748
Administration telephone	19,032
Travel	15,459
Cashier (overage) or shortage	364
Bad debt expense	7,965
Administration, other	35,274
Advertising	21,840
Maintenance supplies	9,165
Maintenance trash	29,303
Maintenance	99,489
Utilities	275,360
House charges, other	49,686
Total controllable expenses	848,133
Total operating expenses	2,489,186
Contribution to profits	5,475,625
Uncontrollable expenses	1,590,392
House profit	$3,885,233

mat in Exhibit 1. The hotel example in the exhibit has 297 rooms for rent 365 days a year, and an annual occupancy rate of 80 percent for the most recent year. (Occupancy is the number of rooms occupied divided by the total rooms available.) This occupancy level is above average but not exceptional. Ninety percent of the revenues come from room rentals. There are four classes of expenses: cost of goods sold, payroll, controllable, and uncontrollable.

BLT monitors performances at the property (i.e., hotel) and corporate (all properties managed for a chain) levels to ensure the owners' long-term objectives are being met. Presently, BLT manages a portfolio of 26 hotels with annual sales of $278 million. This sales volume represents substantial growth during the last decade when the company started with twelve hotels and $63 million in annual revenues. BLT's board of directors, consisting of all shareholders of BLT, wants sales to grow at the rate of 15 percent per year for the next decade with hotel profitability maintained at the current levels. The board also wants BLT-managed hotels to outperform competitors. Although BLT-managed hotels are doing well, they are not meeting the expectation of the board, i.e.:

- they are **not** in the top 20 percent in guest scores and profitability,
- the turnover rate of hourly employees is **not** less than 60 percent annually,
- the turnover rate of managers is **not** less than 20 percent annually,
- budgets are **not** always achieved, and
- owners' unlevered returns on investment are **not** always equal to or greater than 15 percent.

More specifically, the BLT committee agreed on two financial measures for the balanced scorecard. The first indicator was a yield index that gauges a property's revenue per available room (RevPAR) relative to competitive hotels as well as to year-over-year improvement. The inherent objective is to achieve both higher RevPAR levels and faster RevPAR growth rates than those of competitors. The second indicator is an index of operating performance relative to a flexible budget. Rather than focus on property-profit achievement relative to budget, the committee designed this index, which is part of the operating statement in Exhibit 1, to consider only expenses that are controllable by hotel general managers and simultaneously adjusts expected performance to account for variances in business volume (occupancy). The committee called this a flow-through model, and with it they expected the following objectives:

- achieve budget targets,
- superior financial management of hotels,
- outperform competitors in profitability and expense-control,
- achieve internal consistency in property operations, and
- deliver high investment returns to owners.

The committee was particularly pleased with the flow-through model's ability to re-forecast controllable costs using a fixed and variable cost model to adjust performance expectations to reflect actual room rentals. Line items that vary with respect to occupancy are re-forecasted every period that actual occupancy differs from budgeted occupancy. The result is a line item entitled "contribution to house profit from controllable items." This line item incorporates expenditures over which the general manager has considerable control, e.g., payroll, utilities, maintenance, office supplies. However, it does not include items over which the general manager has little or no control, e.g., franchise fees, health and welfare insurance, travel-agent commissions. The advantage of excluding uncontrollable items is that general managers can be held to a higher level of accountability for items that they control without facing the frustration of unanticipated changes to uncontrollable items.

An additional benefit of the flow-through model as a management tool is that it allows owners to focus on management and cost control issues that might otherwise be buried within the financial operating statement. Those factors are exposed in the variance calculations for each line item that is under management control.

The committee recognized that measuring operating performance strictly on financial measures is inconsistent with the long-term investment horizon and with BLT's corporate objectives. Furthermore, they repeatedly noted that financial measures are lagging indicators rather than leading indicators and cannot be used to predict future performance. BLT needs, according to the committee, measures that track financial results while simultaneously monitoring progress in building the capability and acquiring the intangible assets needed for future growth. The committee agreed that the balanced scorecard must have the following characteristics: not limited to financial performance; nonfinancial performance measures dealing with factors important for long-term growth and value creation; inclusion of factors that lead to growth, profitability, and physical maintenance; simple to monitor; and easy for general managers to understand and accept.

Customer Perspective

The committee reviewed the following potential guest-related indicators: customer satisfaction, customer retention, new-customer acquisition, market segmentation, market share, customer profitability, responsiveness, associate knowledge and service levels, and mystery-guest assessments.

Internal research found that guest scores correlate with investment returns, thus substantiating the value to owners of high guest-satisfaction levels. Properties that scored in the top 20 percent of guest-satisfaction scores provided investment returns averaging 17.4 percent in the most recent year. Properties that scored in the top 40 percent of the guest-satisfaction scores still managed a 15.2 percent, while properties below median levels provided only a 12.7 percent return.

Internal Business Processes

The committee evaluated a number of internal business process measures that might bear on the objectives of both management and owners, including the following: associate-productivity rates, service errors and failure rates, maintenance of physical assets, capital-expenditure efficiency, accounting and internal-control practices, and time required to complete key processes and tasks, e.g., check-in, maintenance, breakfast seating and serving.

BLT predominantly manages national franchise affiliations, thus general managers have only minimal control over the matters relating to marketing and brand recognition. Furthermore, a number of the indicators dealing with efficiency and productivity rates are indirectly reflected in the financial flow-through model. The committee developed a comprehensive hotel audit program to check and verify that general managers comply with the internal business process expectations or standards. These criteria are shown in Exhibit 2. Each audit is to be conducted by a manager of internal audit against a detailed check list of items. If there is compliance to all items, the hotel (i.e., its general manager) receives a perfect control of 100 points. Hotels receiving less than 90 points are expected to have serious operating shortcomings. Only with more than 97.5 points will general managers be excused from remedial actions.

Learning and Growth

The committee considered the following possible measures to gauge the learning and growth: personal growth of associates (employees); internal promotion levels; associate satisfaction; associate retention; associate empowerment; strategic skills

---

EXHIBIT 2: OUTLINE OF BLT CONSOLIDATED PROCESS AUDIT

Human-resources best practices

1. Personnel files are properly maintained, e.g., reviews, discipline, tax forms
2. Associates adhere to training schedules
3. Uniforms are worn per policy
4. Hotel complies with provincial and federal human resources regulations

Hotel-improvement best practices

1. Associates are aware of mission statement, critical success factors
2. Guest rooms and public areas are properly cleaned and inspected
3. Defects and guest complaints are properly recorded and resolved
4. Sales and marketing goals are posted and results tracked properly.
5. Hotel adheres to accounting and internal-control processes

Maintenance best practices

1. Guest rooms and public areas are refreshed with quarterly preventive maintenance
2. Major equipment items are maintained according to schedule
3. Inspections are kept current, e.g., fire, elevator, health
4. Pool readings are conducted and logged correctly
5. Capital-expenditure file is maintained correctly

---

of associates, managers, and the organization; training levels and cycle times; cross-training levels of associates and line manager; information technology use; access to strategic information; new initiatives explored or implemented; and community participation and knowledge exhibited by general managers.

Other Concerns

With a median associate turnover rate of 88.3 percent, BLT experienced many personnel issues common to the hospitality industry. That level of turnover meant the company was constantly replacing workers, spending time and energy on training, and experiencing reduced guest-satisfaction levels because of mistakes made by inexperienced associates. Thus, associate (employee) retention presented the greatest opportunity for improvement

within the organization. Furthermore, the committee determined that many of the other measures, although valid, would be ineffective in the absence of a stable base of long-term associates. A supplemental analysis showed that hotels with associate turnover below 100 percent (which is still substantial) enjoyed generally higher profit and RevPAR growth than those with turnover levels exceeding 100 percent. Given the negative impact of associate turnover, the committee recommended that the balanced scorecard emphasize the reduction in turnover levels.

Required: As the management accountant and a member of the balanced scorecard committee, use the case approach to complete the balanced scorecard for BLT.

Clearwater Small Appliances

Clearwater manufactures a wide range of small household appliances such as coffee makers, can openers, microwave and toaster ovens, irons and ironing boards. In 50 years of existence, it has prospered and established a well-respected brand name. Business has been good — at least up to now. Recent changes in methods of retailing require Clearwater to alter significantly its way of doing business. Traditionally, Clearwater has supplied retailers such as department stores, hardware stores, and discount stores. They now are suffering declining sales because giant category retailers like Home Depot, Canadian Tire, Wal-Mart, and Zellers dominate the market. These "power retailers" use sophisticated information and inventory management. Their finely tuned selections, and competitive pricing crowd out weaker retailers. The forecast is that category retailers will continue gaining market share.

So powerful have category retailers become that they tell even the largest and most powerful manufacturers what goods to make, in what colours and sizes, and how much to ship and when. In fact, they dictate practically all terms of business with their suppliers. Some category retailers even charge the manufacturers for shipment errors. They constantly squeeze costs; for example, some have operating and selling expenses as low as 15 percent of sales compared to 28 percent for traditional department stores. The difference is even greater than these 13 percentage points as the sales prices are about 5 percent lower for the category retailers than for department stores.

In order to survive, Clearwater must supply category stores; to be a supplier, Clearwater must tailor its products to please individual category retailers and meet high standards for on time, defect-free merchandise. However, Clearwater wants to preserve its brand name "Clearwater" instead of merely manufacturing store brands. Supplying category retailers is, for Clearwater, only a coping strategy. It recognizes that it needs to supply the category retailers, but it also recognizes that to

survive Clearwater must have a separate and strong identity.

The management team developed a new strategy. In formulating it, they sought substantial input from all parts of Clearwater. As well, buyers and executives from three of the largest category retailers provided insights about what changes would be required to meet their needs. The result is the following internal statement endorsed by the board of directors.

Tactics for Coping With Category Retailers

- **Protect our brands.** If customers ask for our products by name, the category retailers are more likely to stock our products. Consequently, we must advertise and not merely depend on the category retailers for exposure.

- **Customize.** Meet customer requirements — whether category retailer or customer.

- **Innovate constantly.** Non-distinguishable products are vulnerable because category retailers can readily replace suppliers or contract for the manufacture of their own brands.

- **Organize around the category retailer.** The organization will reorganize into multi-disciplinary teams, each of which will serve the largest category retailers.

- **Invest in technology.** The category retailers demand the latest information technology to ensure that the right products arrive on the shelves at the right time.

- **Cut the fat.** If we do not constantly reduce our costs and pass the savings on to the category retailers, they will find manufacturers that can and do.

You, as the vice president controller, with the management team, have been fully involved in formulating the strategy by which to become a profitable supplier to category retailers. You are now to develop an information system for planning (i.e., budgeting one to three years into the future) and monitoring the strategy. This information is to be incorporated into the monthly cost of quality report, which operation you are also to review and make any necessary changes to improve its usefulness.

Cost of Quality Report

Prevention

Quality engineering
Receiving inspection
Quality training

Appraisal

Product inspection

Internal Failures

Scrap
Rework

External Failures

Net cost of returned products

The cost of quality report is compiled monthly by the production vice president and one of the production scheduling engineers using estimates based on their experience. Separate tracking and budgeting do not occur for these costs. The production vice-president is responsible for quality, but many of her subordinates are in better positions for ensuring it.

Required Undertake your project and report your findings to the management committee.

Coffee Maker Supreme

Coffee Maker Supreme (CMS) has been in the business of manufacturing coffee makers for three generations. During the first and second generations the growth in demand was modestly positive, and customers seemed to have been more content with product range and quality. During the time of the present generation of owners, the demand for coffee machines grew at a much higher rate. That demand does not appear to be declining in the foreseeable future. Moreover, customers have become increasingly demanding for specialized and high-quality coffee makers.

Background

CMS is a privately owned manufacturer and distributor of machines to make coffee. Sales are more than $200 million per year. Customers — from all parts of world — are restaurants, cafes, and cafeterias. Sales are made by commissioned sales representatives supported by a Web site to process orders and to provide after-sales service. CMS started in the Canadian market, but expanded into the United States a decade before the free-trade agreement. Nicole Roberto joined the business after completing her CMA. Two years earlier, she had completed her undergraduate degree in business. She encouraged her father to purchase coffee machine manufacturers in France and Italy in order to expand into the European market. She then spent a decade in Europe developing the business. Her heritage language — Italian — and her French immersion studies from grades 1 to 12 assisted her in successfully developing the European business.

In 1997, the sales representatives from around the world were provided with Web-based sales support for transacting sales and for the customers to obtain post-sales service and support. This system proved highly successful, allowing CMS to further expand into Europe and into the Japanese and Mexican markets. The global reach with plants in Canada, U.S., France and Italy meant that there was a rather haphazard product line. The four

plants produced 27 products of which 10 were literally duplicates of another 10, resulting in only 17 truly different products. In 2000, the product line was rationalized allowing two of the plants to be closed, and for the product line to be increased by 13 new coffee makers that were different from existing products. Of the current 30 different coffee makers, 16 are manufactured in one plant and 14 are manufactured in the other. In effect, the new products expanded both ends of the product line, i.e., both larger-capacity and small special-purpose coffee makers. Moreover, features were added to make all coffee makers more versatile. In effect, each of the 30 products experienced product design and manufacturing process changes.

Global sourcing was introduced at the same time to ensure procurement of the most appropriate and cost-effective materials and components. Along with global sourcing, the decades-old practice of 100 percent inspection was replaced with a more modern system of random checks. This allowed for most of the inspectors to be reassigned. Suppliers were responsible for quality of all materials and components, and manufacturing workers were responsible for quality control in the manufacturing process. Each worker knew the operating specifications, and if a unit received at his or her station was not up to standard, the manufacturing process could be stopped for the necessary corrections.

Performance Reports

The financial results of the first full year of operations with the product line and related changes are shown in Exhibit 1. These results were what president Nicole Roberto showed you as you started your first day as the controller. Nicole had been brought back to Canada three months earlier when the previous president had been obliged to retire for health reasons.

The first task assigned to you by Nicole was to determine why, when sales targets were met, operating income was substantially lower than budget.

EXPANSION

EXHIBIT 1: OPERATING STATEMENT

(millions of dollars)

	Budget	Actual	Variance
Sales	$216.0	$218.3	$ 2.3
Cost of Goods Sold			
Variable costs:			
Materials	62.7	64.8	(2.1)
Manufacturing labour	10.6	11.4	(0.8)
Manufacturing overhead	23.7	25.1	(1.4)
Selling	8.6	8.7	(0.1)
	105.6	110.0	(4.4)
Contribution Margin	110.4	108.3	(2.1)
Fixed Expenses			
Manufacturing overhead	49.4	66.1	(16.7)
Selling	10.7	10.6	0.1
Administration	18.6	18.7	(0.1)
	78.7	95.4	(16.7)
Operating Income	$ 31.7	$ 12.9	$(18.8)

EXHIBIT 2: COST OF QUALITY REPORT

(millions of dollars)

	2001	2000	1999	1998	1997	1996
Prevention costs	$ 1.2	$3.1	$3.2	$3.0	$2.8	$2.6
Appraisal costs	0.1	1.3	1.4	1.2	1.0	1.0
Internal failure costs	2.1	1.1	1.0	0.7	0.8	0.8
External failure costs	6.7	0.6	0.2	0.6	0.3	0.4
Total quality costs	$10.1	6.1	5.8	5.5	4.9	4.8

EXHIBIT 3: CUSTOMER SATISFACTION SURVEY

(December surveys, % score on a 0% to 100% scale)

	2001	2000	1999	1998	1997	1996
Product quality	61.5	85.5	84.7	85.9	86.1	85.3
Durability	58.3	93.3	92.7	92.2	92.7	93.6
Good value	48.6	75.1	77.5	76.6	78.1	76.4
Features	88.6	53.8	56.3	55.8	54.7	53.1

You first reviewed the variances. The sales variance at one percent was trivial. After talking to the manufacturing vice-president, who was in charge of both plants, you concluded that the material variance is largely attributed to some yield problems with some materials and components, and that these yield problems created the unfavourable variances for direct labour and variable manufacturing overhead. A bigger problem was the fixed manufacturing overhead. The manufacturing vice-president explained this variance to be the result of charging to fixed manufacturing overhead, the rework required in getting the plants accustomed to manufacturing the new and newly designed products. Warranty work was also charged to fixed manufacturing overhead, whether an actual or estimated charge. You also asked for and received the cost of quality report (Exhibit 2) and the customer satisfaction survey results (Exhibit 3).

Required As the controller, carry out your assignment using the case approach.

CASE 6

Consolidated Pump

PRODUCT DIFFERENTION

Your firm, Consolidated Pump, is a major manufacturer and distributor of industrial pumps. Due to technological advances in pump design and manufacturing, sales and profits have grown substantially. Other firms, observing this growth, have entered or expanded their presence in the pump market, and consequently competition has intensified. See Exhibits 1 and 2 for the impact of recent competition on financial performance.

The technological advances have been applicable to a wide range of pumps, and Consolidated Pump has purchased several previously autonomous pump manufacturers that produced related products. Consolidated Pump then improved the technology of its pumps and its manufacturing

processes. As a result, Consolidated Pump now produces 87 different products. The number of inventoried parts for making pumps has grown more rapidly than has the number of assembled pumps. Because of the large number of different parts, the purchasing department costs have grown at a particularly rapid rate. This has been a concern, and the financial analyst studied these costs. Exhibit 3 shows this analysis.

The standard price equals total cost plus a markup of 80 percent. Product costs equal direct materials, direct labour, and overhead allocated on direct labour hours. In the past, this pricing practice has been satisfactory. Due to near total automation of production, direct labour

---

EXHIBIT 1: SUMMARY OF FINANCIAL STATEMENTS

CONSOLIDATED PUMP

(in millions of dollars)

	1998	1999	2000	2001
Sales	$69	$81	$95	$112
Less:				
Variable manufacturing cost of goods sold	22	18	18	15
Variable marketing and administrative costs	4	6	7	8
Total variable costs	26	24	25	23
Contribution margin	43	57	70	89
Deduct:				
Fixed manufacturing costs	18	27	34	50
Fixed marketing and administrative costs	16	20	24	27
Total fixed costs	34	47	58	77
Operating income	9	10	12	12
Net income after taxes	$ 5	$ 6	$ 7	$ 7
Inventories	10	19	23	29
Total assets	39	43	48	50
Long-term bonds	21	23	19	17
Owners' equity	9	12	19	24

EXHIBIT 2: CONSOLIDATED PUMP'S COMPARATIVE PERFORMANCE DATA

(as a percentage of industry total)

	Sales	Net Income	Total Assets	Owners' Equity
1990	4.7	5.1	4.5	5.2
1991	4.9	5.3	4.6	5.5
1992	4.7	5.4	4.7	5.4
1993	4.8	5.9	4.5	5.9
1994	4.9	6.0	5.0	5.8
1995	5.0	6.4	5.1	6.4
1996	6.0	7.2	6.2	7.0
1997	6.4	7.1	6.2	7.4
1998	7.0	8.5	6.8	7.7
1999	7.2	12.4	7.7	9.5
2000	8.6	13.1	7.9	10.2
2001	9.5	11.4	7.9	10.3

EXHIBIT 3: ANALYSIS OF CONSOLIDATED PUMP'S PURCHASING DEPARTMENT

Senior management has been concerned that costs have increased at an alarming rate in the purchasing department, although the director of purchasing regularly overworks her purchasing agents. The analysis sought to identify the causes of the growth in purchasing department costs and then understand how to control those factors. As a first step, the analyst asked purchasing people what were the reasons for their activities. Although 11 cost drivers were initially identified, after analysis, the director reasoned that three cost drivers were significant: sales, number of different pumps, and number of different parts.

Multiple regression was initially used on the 12 years of data, but multi-collinearity was greater than 0.8. Below are the results from simple regression for three cost drivers (independent variables) and purchasing department total costs (the dependent variable).

Variable	Coefficient*	Standard Error*
Regression Number 1		
Constant	5,702.1	2,741.3
Independent variable 1:		
Sales in dollars ($r^2 = 0.46$)	1.9	1.2
Regression Number 2		
Constant	2,491.7	1,021.6
Independent variable 1:		
Number of different pumps ($r^2 = 0.32$)	61.4	70.3
Regression Number 3		
Constant	40.4	25.8
Independent variable 1:		
Number of different parts ($r^2 = 0.79$)	5.9	1.6

* Elimination of some zeros for the coefficients and standard errors, did not distort the relationships between respective coefficient and standard error.

is now only 9 percent of manufacturing costs. Materials are about 10 percent. The remaining 81 percent comes from manufacturing overhead. Senior management has become suspicious of the allocation of overhead based on direct labour; a detailed study of activities found that time in production was a more valid indicator of the manufacturing overhead consumed by a product than direct

---

EXHIBIT 4: ALLOCATION OF CONSOLIDATED PUMP'S COSTS, PRODUCT PRICING

The 87 pumps made by Consolidated Pump can be aggregated into five classes. The cost of an individual pump is a variation of its class reflecting more or fewer materials and processing time. The idea of a class of pump simplifies production and marketing.

	Class				
	A	**B**	**C**	**D**	**E**
Standard Unit Costs					
Direct Labour	$ 4.22	$ 6.17	$ 7.87	$ 10.48	$ 14.69
Materials	3.40	5.10	6.07	7.92	9.74
Overhead*	31.68	42.24	50.69	71.81	107.71
	$39.30	$53.51	$ 64.63	$ 90.21	$132.14
Consolidated's Standard Price	$70.74	$96.32	$116.33	$162.38	$237.85
Competitors Price	$69.00	$93.00	$114.00	$170.00	$240.00
Units Sold	51,100	52,400	57,400	411,400	127,400
Direct labour hours, actual	1.5	2.0	2.4	3.4	5.1
Time in (hours) production, actual	5.2	7.1	15.0	18.2	26.5

handwritten: 3.6 5.0 6.7 66.8 30.3

---

* Manufacturing overhead is allocated to products with the following formula:

$$\frac{\text{Budgeted Overhead in dollars}}{\text{Budgeted Direct Labour in hours}} \times \text{actual direct labour hours}$$

---

labour hours. For this alternative approach to assigning manufacturing overhead, you have gathered the preliminary data contained in Exhibit 4. It is unclear about whether there is any value in changing the allocation base.

Parts inventories have been increasing in recent years to where now they are out of control. The annual budget makes provision for a parts inventory based on last year, with adjustments for changes to the product line to be assembled. This approach to inventory planning has led to excesses for some parts and shortages for others. However,

the nature of the pump business is that pumps manufactured and shipped represent firm orders. For most pumps, demand is highly predictable and parts are readily available within one to two days. However, the higher-priced pumps, are more difficult to forecast.

Required The controller asked you, a management accountant, to (1) identify the reasons for profit problems through quantitative and qualitative analysis, and (2) recommend solutions.

handwritten notes:

JIT INVENTORY FOR ALL PARTS
↳ DISSATISFIED CUSTOMERS
↳ LOSS SALES.
31.68 × 1.5

→ COSTS ARE NOT BEING ALLOCATED PROPERLY
→ TIME IN PRODUCTION & DIRECT LABOUR HAS A HUGE DIFF.
→ LACK CORPORATE OBJECTIVES

KAIZEN - CONTINUOUS SYSTEM
↳ REDUCE COSTS
↳ TRACK BETTER

→ EST BETTER RELATIONSHIP w/ SUPPLIERS
↳ MAYBE OWN SUPPLIERS OUT

Container Plastics Company

Ron Forlani has just gone public and expanded his container business. As a creative and skilled engineer, Ron develops technologically advanced machinery and moulds, which provide Container Plastics with a competitive advantage. Above average profits come from the technological advantages, but only temporarily as competitor imitation takes between six months and one year.

Ron has two tactics for addressing this technology copying. First, he plans and works towards continuously introducing technological improvements in processes and products. For example, there is an ongoing goal for production costs to decrease 8 percent a year. Second, Container Plastics stresses new products. For example, there is a policy that 25 percent of the sales each year must come from products introduced in the past five years.

Container Plastics is in the plastic products industry, specifically in the rigid packaging sector. Its products include pop bottles, cosmetic jars, beverage cases, dairy cups and tubs, food trays, pails, and oil containers. In the industry, there are constant modifications and improvements in machinery and processes. Technology is becoming an increasingly important competitive factor in productivity as are product quality and performance. The industry is being pressed to increase the use of higher-performance polymer materials, instrumentation, controls and automated materials-handling techniques in its processing operations. While these technologies continue to be generally available, they are more demanding in their implementation, and operation and maintenance, reflecting a greater need for higher levels of labour and management skills. Such skills are generally scarce. This is not so with Container Plastics.

Container Plastics is one of the few Canadian organizations that have developed extensive research and development capabilities. The Canadian market was not large enough. However, the free-trade agreement with United States, and the reduction in the tariff barrier that protected Canadian rigid packaging organizations, has forced Container Plastics to compete in a larger market.

In this larger market, competition is aggressive and persistent. In addition, waste disposal difficulties with plastics has placed pressure on the industry for solutions. Container Plastics and its competitors have reduced the amount of plastics used in given applications and developed means for economically recycling plastic materials. Additionally, the trade association, the Society of the Plastic Industry of Canada, has a very active program to educate the public about the role of plastics in the environment and to implement viable technologies in Canada that will reduce the amount of plastic materials that eventually reside in landfill sites.

The performance advantages of plastics over competitive products, assures their status as a material of choice in a wide range of applications. Because of evolving global marketing strategies, including rationalization, and tougher competition due to lower tariffs, the industry will not maintain the past rate of growth. Nevertheless, the growth rate will continue to exceed that for the Canadian manufacturing sector.

A technological advantage of Container Plastics is that production set-up can be done relatively quickly and inexpensively. Consequently, five basic moulding machines produce nearly 100 different products. This is a sharp improvement from earlier technology which would have required 20 or more moulding machines.

Ron wants accurate product costing for profitable expansion. As the organization is new, he believes the time is appropriate for developing a costing system that is accurate and efficient. Ron has some understanding of job-order and process costing systems and standard costing, but he does not know what to use as the organization grows.

You have learned the following about Container Plastics:

- There is a sales staff of eight persons, who are located throughout Ontario, Quebec, and Northeastern United States. Agents are employed in Atlantic Canada.

- Sales persons contact clients, former clients, and prospective clients for orders. With product design engineers and the production scheduling manager, the sales person prepares a quotation.

- Generally, an order is for a certain quantity of a specified product. It will be for a future period, generally a year, with delivery being on a regular schedule or as requested if the client organization uses a JIT inventory system.

- Product pricing is a markup of 1200 percent over cost, which is calculated as direct materials. All other costs are indirect. The markup gets reduced if necessary to obtain an order. Ron must approve all "markdowns," which he does automatically if the sales person requests.

- As long production runs reduce set-up costs, products are often inventoried for clients. There is no charge for this service.

The indirect manufacturing costs are many times larger than the materials costs, as shown below. With 27 months of data, you run simple regressions to understand what drives the various indirect cost categories. Exhibits 1 and 2 show the operating statement and the regression equations, respectively.

To maintain leading-edge technology, new equipment is being constantly considered. All proposed equipment for more than $10,000 is subject to capital budgeting evaluation. An example follows. Ron is concerned about whether the current

---

EXHIBIT 1

CONTAINER PLASTICS COMPANY
Operating Statement
For the Year Ended December 31, 2001

Revenue		$43,152,750
Expenses:		
Materials	4,226,740	
Machine room	15,071,788	
Warehouse	5,877,224	
Set up	1,548,119	
Shipping	1,122,487	
Engineering	1,740,821	
Administration	1,950,298	
Selling and marketing	3,477,844	35,015,321
Operating income		$ 8,137,429

EXHIBIT 2

	Dependent Variable	Independent Variable	Constant	Slope
1.	Set-up costs	Number of set-ups	$ 97,869	$2,721
2.	Set-up costs	Number of orders	154,872	482
3.	Warehouse costs	Square feet	769,072	7
4.	Warehouse costs	Size of order	319,543	0.54
5.	Shipping costs	Size of order	54,912	1.23
6.	Shipping costs	Number of shipments	24,108	374
7.	Machine room costs	Through-put time	671,564	119
8.	Machine room costs	Machine time	974,653	197

Note: For the constant or intercept, the t-value was equal to or greater than 2 for above equations 2, 4, and 5, and less than 2 for the others. For the slope or beta, the t-value was equal to or greater than 2 for equations 1, 3, 6, and 7, and less than 2 for the others.

approach is consistent with accepted NPV practices.

Cost of equipment	($20,000,000)
Reduction in costs ($2,500,000 per year after income taxes for the 5-year life of the equipment; $2,500,000 × 3.791)	9,478,000
Increased sales ($2,000,000 per year less 30% variable costs and income taxes at 40% for the 5-year life of the equipment; $2,000,000 × 0.7 × 0.6 × 3.791)	3,184,000
Debt financing	6,000,000
Working capital	(1,000,000)
Tax shield from equipment ($20,000,000 × 0.29)	5,800,000
Salvage value ($4,000,000 at the end of year 5; $4,000,000 × 0.3222)	1,289,000
NPV	$ 4,751,000

$$\text{Tax Shield Rate} = \frac{T \times C}{C + R} \frac{2 + R}{2(1 + R)}$$

where,

T = the income tax rate
C = the CCA rate
R = the cost of capital or required rate of return

Required As the new controller hired to make Container Plastics a world class organization, use the case approach to put forth recommendations for a cost system that will help in accurately pricing quotations. Also, you are to make recommendations, if necessary, for improving the capital budgeting process.

CASE 8

Digital-Imaging Robots

You and your sister have a good business idea. No, upon reflection, it not a good business idea, it is a great idea. You had 15 years experience with robotics with an automotive manufacturer. Your sister had a decade doing digital imaging research. Together the two of you have designed the next generation of industrial robots, complete with patents and firm outstanding orders for at least three years. The essence of your business model is the advanced control module which is placed in a standard robot. Money does not seem to be a problem, with all the offers from angels (rich investors who provide money and advice to startup businesses), VCs (venture capitalists), and IPO (initial public offering) specialists.

For a start, you and your sister envisage manufacturing 10,000 robots a year in a 50,000 square foot plant in Lethbridge, Alberta. Three hundred production workers will be needed to work on two shifts. The number of maintenance employees are expected to be 50. The most important group — of engineers, programmers and systems analysts — will be those 35 involved with the research, design, development and production of the control modules for the robots. As there are a limited number of firms with advanced robotic manufacturing operations, five sales engineers will be sufficient as long as they have an equal number of support staff. Accounting and other administrative staff are expected to number 45. That set-up with improvements in productivity would allow for production to increase by 10 to 15 percent a year over a decade. Adding a third shift would increase capacity by a further 40 percent. Details are shown in Exhibit 1.

To get the business going, you have been looking for a building. There is one that appears to meet your current criteria. Your real estate agent (i.e., your mother-in-law) wants you to sign for the building before it is "off the market"; she says it is a unique opportunity. However, you are not sure about making the commitment right now, despite the agent's persistence.

The management team will be headed by you as president and chief executive officer. Your sister will be the chairperson and the vice-president of research. Two vice-presidents will need to be hired, one for production, and the other for sales. Since your wife, a chartered accountant, was just fired from her job as a tax auditor she could be the vice-president, finance and administration, as well as the CFO. Your sister's husband, a graduate in human resources, could be the vice-president, human resources; his problem with authority figures would unlikely inhibit his performance.

As you and your sister work on the budget numbers for the new firm, you decide to visit the university from which you graduated in the hope of talking to one of your professors. Fortunately, he was in his office and he remembers you, and asks if you are still bullish on Dome Petroleum. (You had forgotten that recommendation. You sure believed in Jack Gallager. Too bad Dome Petroleum stock became worthless.) The office seems smaller than you remember, there are more books, but the professor, except for less hair, has changed little in 15 years. Teaching must provide a good life. You quickly explain your business plans and show him the numbers, as in Exhibit 1. Over the next hour, he asks you many questions. For some of the questions, you have answers, but for others, you do not. At 6:45 pm, he says, "I must teach in 15 minutes. Can you and your sister meet me in my office tomorrow evening."

At the meeting on the following day, he says the following:

> Your strategy is to produce leading-edge industrial robots. Your competitive advantage is with the design stage. You are able to incorporate the latest research into the functioning of robots. However, this is but one activity in the value chain that leads to industrial customers that believe your robots provide advantages over all

EXHIBIT 1: OPERATING BUDGET, FIRST YEAR (Millions)

	Year 1	Description
Sales	$165.00	10,000 robots times $16,500 each
Annual labour costs		
Production	$ 18.00	300 employees times $60,000
Production maintenance	3.50	50 employees times $70,000
Research and design	3.50	35 employees times $100,000
Sales — outside	0.50	5 employees times $100,000
Sales — inside	0.20	5 employees times $40,000
Accounting, administration	2.70	45 employees times $60,000
Other production costs	6.00	approximately 40 percent of labour costs
	$ 34.40	
Other annual costs		
Executives	2.00	fixed overhead
Production	10.50	variable overhead, fixed overhead
Production maintenance	5.00	variable and fixed costs
Research and design	5.00	fixed costs
Sales	1.00	variable and fixed costs
Accounting, administration	2.00	fixed costs
Building, property maintenance	0.50	50,000 square feet times $10 per square foot
Miscellaneous other costs	6.00	approximately 40 percent of other annual costs
	32.00	
Operating income	$ 98.60	
Capital assets		
Building	$ 15.50	land and building, amortization included in the operating statement
Production equipment	$ 55.00	amortization included in the operating statement
Production maintenance equipment	10.00	amortization included in the operating statement
Research and design equipment	16.00	amortization included in the operating statement
Sales equipment	1.00	amortization included in the operating statement
Accounting, administration	2.00	amortization included in the operating statement
Leasehold improvements	6.00	amortization included in the operating statement
Working capital	24.00	
	$129.50	

[handwritten] MANUFACTURING? KEEP IT OR NOT?

[handwritten] * HOLD THEM ACCOUNTABLE TO THE PPL YOU OUTSOURCE WITH.

competitor robots. You must design all other activities in the chain so that they too achieve world-class performance. Consider outsourcing or application service providers for those activities for which you do not have a competitive advantage. You and your sister must decide if either or both of you will be active in management, or remain as designers and owners. Also, hire employees based on merit, not family connections.

Consider your situation as a case question; and prepare for me a case response. Then I could be me more explicit in addressing your proposed business undertaking.

He also provides you with information about Dell Computer which makes extensive use of outsourcing, almost everything from sales to manufacturing including research and development. Dell's business model invested significantly in supplier assets, which it then linked to its customer assets using the Internet and its organizational know-how and systems. Consequently, Dell enables customers to access sales and service on its Web site. Its network of linked suppliers makes it possible for the company to efficiently tailor PC products to fit the needs of individual buyers, whether for home use or for a global company.

He explains that Dell was quick to become Web-based for sales and customer service operations. It has no traditional distribution network standing between itself and its customers. Customers are served by a telephone or an on-line order taker who actually works for a division of a telephone company. More frequently, the orders are placed by the customer via Dell's Web page. Once placed by telephone or Internet, the order is sent to a coordinator — actually an employee who works for another company — who in turn passes the order to the relevant Dell assembly plant from among five around the world. At the same time, the coordinator directs the suppliers to ship the parts to the selected plant. The coordinator also directs the parcel courier to the respective plant at the predetermined time to pick up and then deliver the finished computer to the customer.

Moreover, Dell depends on its ability to optimize all assets that make up its business model, including relationships with employees, suppliers, investors, and customers. This clarity of business model is reflected in Dell's above average financial performance.

Required Prepare a case response, as requested by the professor.

Dindal Air Conditioners

Dindal is a manufacturer of air conditioners for the North American market. It sells the Dindal brand through independent agents and produces units with the brand names of various retailers. Although largely an assembler of purchased parts at this time, Dindal does produce its own condensers. It also sells condensers to other manufacturers of air conditioners. Consequently, it has two operating divisions, condenser manufacturing and air conditioner assembly.

Once Dindal produced nearly all of its own components. However, over the last 20 years, it has gradually switched from making components to buying them. Now it makes only a single component, the condenser. The switching to purchased parts was done gradually. Dindal wanted to make only those parts for which it had distinct competitive and strategic advantages.

The Dindal condensers and air conditioners are durable, efficient, and competitively priced. These product characteristics have been crucial for success, and they require efficient labour, competitively priced and high-quality parts, mistake-free assembly, minimal inventories, and on-time

---

EXHIBIT 1

DINDAL AIR CONDITIONERS, CONDENSER DIVISION
Operating Statement
For the Year Ending December 31, 2001
(in thousands of dollars)

REVENUE		
Outside sales		$27,500
Assembly division		22,500
		50,000
VARIABLE EXPENSES		
Manufacturing	21,000	
Administration	3,000	
Selling	3,000	27,000
FIXED EXPENSES		
Manufacturing	7,000	
Selling, administration	3,000	
Research and development	2,500	12,500
OPERATING INCOME		$10,500

Division Balance Sheet

Working capital		$ 4,000
Net fixed assets		26,000
Investment		$30,000

DINDAL AIR CONDITIONERS, ASSEMBLY DIVISION
Operating Statement
For the Year Ending December 31, 2001
(in thousands of dollars)

REVENUE	
Dindal brand	$30,000
Other brands	22,000
	52,000
COST OF GOODS SOLD	31,000
GROSS MARGIN	21,000
ADMINISTRATIVE EXPENSES	7,000
SELLING EXPENSES	10,000
OPERATING INCOME	$ 4,000

Division Balance Sheet

Working capital	$ 6,000
Net fixed assets	36,000
Investment	$42,000

deliveries. Also, to remain successful the condenser division has an active research and product development team that is responsible for improving the products and manufacturing processes.

Once a year, the board of directors reviews divisional performance and assesses the company's future opportunities and threats. This is an informal occasion, but the directors — especially those with significant share holdings — are very serious about understanding the operations and obtaining improved results. At this year's meeting, the directors were again unhappy with the performance of the assembly division. That division's general manager explained the poor performance as a consequence of the transfer price. The directors asked for a justification of the transfer price method and for regularly produced non-financial information on the performance of both divisions. You, as the president to whom the general managers report, have taken upon yourself to resolve the board's concerns.

You first recognize that profitability of Dindal and its divisions has been positive and over the last few years largely comparable to the attached financial statements for the recent year. Each division reports as a profit centre, and the condenser division is clearly superior. Perhaps because of this unevenness of profitability, there is a dispute between the general managers of the two divisions. The condenser general manager wants a market-based transfer price. The assembly general manager wants it to be actual cost of goods sold plus 50 percent.

In reviewing the transfer price, you note that it is set at the average market price for long-term contracts to other assemblers of air conditioners. For the latest year, Dindal sold 110,000 condensers to outside customers, while the assembly division purchased 90,000 condensers. The assembly division sold 50,000 Dindal air conditioners, and 40,000 under other brand names. The bonus set by the directors last year was equal to 30 percent of a general manager's salary if their division's ROI exceeds 18 percent. The ROI is operating income divided by divisional investment. It was 35 percent for the condenser division for the latest year, but only 9.5 percent for the assembly division.

Required As the president, prepare a report to the board of directors that addresses and resolves their concerns.

Electronic Process Equipment

Tom Simon developed a process control system in the early 1970s for an independent pulp and paper mill on Vancouver Island. He had been hired as the shift engineer, but realized that many of the operational problems at the mill could be solved with improved process controls. Although he had not set out to develop a process control system, he developed numerous individual process controls before he understood that the integration of all process controls into a system would improve the mill's operational efficiency and effectiveness. After designing and implementing the world's first integrated process control system for a pulp and paper mill, he was promoted to chief engineer. However, that did not satisfy Simon's urge to be creative.

In 1977 Simon, with two other young engineers, formed Electronic Process Equipment (EPE) to design, assemble, and implement process control systems for pulp and paper mills. Their first clients were British Columbia pulp and paper mills, then, after incorporating computers for better coordination, process control systems were sold to pulp and paper mills in Eastern Canada, the states of Washington, Oregon, and Georgia, and Norway. Subsequently, EPE expanded to all parts of the world where pulp and paper mills existed. By 1984, EPE was the world's leading process controls consulting engineering firm in the pulp and paper industry. The decision was made at that time to differentiate itself from all competitors by expanding into the research, development, and manufacturer of leading-edge process control equipment. Then, in 1986, EPE expanded by providing process control systems to the petroleum and chemical industries.

Presently, EPE is employee-owned and highly specialized in designing and manufacturing or assembling process control equipment for customers from around the world in the pulp, paper, petroleum, and chemical industries. EPE provides a full process control service from the initial design, to the detailed engineering drawings, to the manufacture or assembly of equipment, and to its installation, testing, and ongoing maintenance.

EPE, as you would expect, has been dominated by engineers. All senior positions were occupied by engineers until 1989 when a chartered accountant was hired to be the vice-president finance. Since then there has been only one accountant among the engineers. Despite competition, EPE is now approaching annual sales of one-half billion dollars, but there have been concerns with the cost accounting system. As a consulting management accountant, you have been requested to evaluate the existing costing system and recommend changes in order that the needs of EPE be met. Your approach to the assignment is to (1) understand the existing system, (2) understand the needs for a cost accounting system, (3) understand the shortcomings of the existing system in regard to the needs, and (4) recommend a cost accounting system that meets those needs.

To understand the existing system, you meet with the vice-president finance who (1) describes the system in general terms, (2) arranges interviews for you with the controller, manager of cost accounting, and manager of budgeting, and (3) provides you with documentation of the existing system. With these sources you piece together descriptions of the existing cost accounting system, needs, and shortcomings.

Existing System

Presently, there is a distributed accounting system that is provided by the same supplier that had been used with the earlier mainframe computer. This system is adequate for valuing inventory for financial reporting purposes and for preparing periodic financial reports. It has common data and account definitions across different business units so that financial managers can readily compare and consolidate financial results across multiple units and divisions. It can prepare complete financial statements shortly after the close of an accounting period that require few, if any, post-closing adjustments. It prepares statements consistent with standards established by financial reporting, government, regulatory, and tax authorities; the system of data recording and processing has excellent integrity so that it satisfies stringent audit and internal control standards.

The existing system also reports individual product costs using variable and fixed cost classifications and responsibility centres used for external financial reporting, to value inventory and to measure cost-of-goods sold. It provides financial feedback to managers and employees on the same reporting cycle used to prepare the aggregate organizational financial statements. The chart of accounts and database capacity allows a wide variety of special reports to be produced on the same basis as the financial reports.

Needs and Shortcomings

You interview all senior managers plus middle managers in cost accounting, sales, and manufacturing. After 13 interviews, you conclude there is unanimous agreement that the existing system is adequately meeting the requirement for financial reporting. Nevertheless, there are two shortcomings with the existing system. First, the system is inadequate in estimating the cost of activities and business processes, and the cost and profitability of products, services, and customers. Second, the system is inadequate in providing useful feedback to improve processes.

The first shortcoming arises from the assignment of costs to products and services. The system uses direct labour hours to allocate indirect and support costs. Direct labour is not appropriate because direct labour is not a high proportion of the company's manufacturing conversion costs. EPE has extensive automatic manufacturing processes. It also has shifted some of the costs of materials acquisition activities (such as purchasing, receiving, inspection, handling, and storage) to a materials overhead pool; those costs are allocated to purchased items based on a percentage markup over purchase cost. To meet the needs of complex processes, multiple products and services, and diverse customers, EPE uses additional allocation bases, like material cost and machine hours. These modifications all assume that manufacturing indirect and support costs vary with the physical volume or number of the units manufactured. They fail to recognize that many expensive manufacturing resources are supplied to handle production of batches of items (activities required for set-up, ordering, receiving, moving, and inspecting products) and to design and sustain the myriad of products the plant is capable of producing (activities required to design, improve, and maintain individual products). The cost system fails to capture the economies of production batches and product variety.

Another particularly devastating loss from the inaccurate cost system is that product designers and developers receive either no information or highly distorted information about the production costs of products they are designing. EPE's costing system forces product designers and developers to use obsolete and distorted information when making design choices and trade-offs. The erroneous choices and trade-offs made during this phase become locked in; they are costly and difficult to change when the actual cost behaviour is revealed during the subsequent manufacturing phase.

The cost system relies on responsibility cost centres for accumulating costs, both primary centres where actual fabrication or assembly production work is performed, and secondary cost centres, such as indirect labour, maintenance, and tooling preparation, that provide services and support to the primary cost centres. But assigning costs to responsibility centres gives little visibility to the costs of performing activities and business processes. Most activities and business processes use resources from many different cost centres. For example, it was noticed that an activity, like *respond to customer requests,* actually involved people from seven different departments. The customer service department, where the company thought this activity was focussed, incurred only about 30 percent of the total cost of performing the total activity. The lack of information about the cost of activities and business processes has impeded EPE in setting priorities for eliminating inefficiencies, and makes it essentially impossible to benchmark activity and business process costs across units, either internal or external to the organization. Consequently, EPE often does not know where to focus total quality and re-engineering initiatives.

The present cost accounting system allocates manufacturing costs to products. However, the extensive costs for marketing, selling, administration, distribution, research and development, and general administration are not assigned at all to cost objects such as products, services, and customers. This is because periodic financial reporting does not require or in fact allow these outlays to be assigned to cost objects. For financial reporting purposes, these cash expenditures are treated as period expenses. No attempt is made to causally link them to the activities and business processes actually being performed or to the cost objects — products, services and customers — that create the demand for or benefits from these expenditures.

As there are no financial accounting requirements at all for allocating indirect and support expenses to services produced or customers served, the service part of EPE's business does not merely suffer from distorted cost numbers; it has no cost numbers at all. There are responsibility centres for services, but there is no understanding of the costs of individual services and the costs by customer.

The second shortcoming is that the existing system does not provide adequate information to support organizational continuous learning and improvement. The present competitive environment requires managers and operators to have timely and accurate information to help them make processes more efficient and more customer-focussed. The existing system prepares and issues summary financial feedback according to a monthly financial reporting cycle. Due to the complexities and adjustments associated with closing the books, the reports are delayed but only for several days after the close of the accounting period which is still too late for responsibility centres to take immediate corrective actions. A production manager remarked:

> To understand the problem of delay and aggregated financial information, you could think of the responsibility centre manager as a bowler, throwing a ball at pins every minute. But we don't let the bowler see how many pins he has knocked down with each throw. At the end of the month we close the books, calculate the total number of pins knocked down during the month, compare this total with a standard, and report the total and the variance back to the bowler. If the total number is below standard, we ask the bowler for an explanation and encourage him to do better next period. We are beginning to understand that we won't turn out many world-class bowlers with this type of reporting system.

In addition, the monthly performance reports for many operating departments contain extensive cost allocations, forcing managers to be held accountable for performance that is neither under their control nor traceable to them. The costs of corporate- or manufacturing-level resources, such as the heat and lighting in the building or the landscaping outside, are allocated arbitrarily to individual departments despite the departments having no responsibility for these costs. For example, referring back to the bowling metaphor, think about the accountants, after a ball is thrown down each of the establishment's 35 lanes, counting every pin knocked down, dividing by 35, and reporting back the average, say 8.25714 to every bowler. The number may be quite accurate (it does represent the mean number of pins knocked down per alley), but it is completely useless to an individual bowler. Each bowler wants to know the number of pins he or she has knocked down in order to improve on the next throw. A number has no value when it is influenced by actions of others who are uncontrollable.

Required Recommend a cost accounting system that meets the needs of EPE. Explain and justify your recommendation.

Government Services

You are the newly appointed deputy minister of a provincial government department. There are 6,000 employees in the department, grouped into a corporate office plus six regions. Each region has a regional director. The corporate office has 400 employees who provide corporate services, policy development, and some centralized services.

Each region is an autonomous unit run by a powerful regional director. The power is in terms of certain political and community support. The minister and his cabinet colleagues want these regional empires reduced in power and brought under your control. There have been problems because the regions have been delivering programs according to the regional directors' wishes, rather than as legislated.

When you explain to the regional directors what you want done in the way of program standardization, they all agree, but nothing changes. You cannot terminate these regional directors because they have many years of service with performance evaluated at excellent for all recent years. The process of documenting poor performance and by that terminating regional directors would take years. These regional directors are all well paid and unlikely to leave on their own. The story circulating is that they do not need to change as you will soon leave, just like your predecessors.

You have a problem. You have promised the minister and the premier that you will standardize program delivery, but the regional directors who must do it for you will not co-operate. You have one year, or be terminated. As an "order-in-council" appointee, the minister can terminate you on short notice. However, you cannot terminate the regional directors the same way as they are appointees of the public service commission. You are at a loss for a solution. Responsibility accounting does not seem to work.

Required With the case approach, put forth alternatives, evaluate their likelihood of success, select the most appropriate, and then suggest an implementation plan.

Home Renovations

You have just become a shareholder of Home Renovations, Inc. Of the outstanding shares, you own 10 percent while Jean Paul Flynn, the founder, owns the remaining 90 percent. Mr. Flynn started Home Renovations 20 years ago with only himself. Now there are 15 permanent salaried employees plus 200 to 300 trades persons on contract for 20 or more hours a week.

You are also the chief financial officer, controller, and office manager. You manage the 5 office staff while Mr. Flynn manages the 10 estimators/project managers.

There is a strong demand for renovations. However, new firms are capturing most of this growth. Mr. Flynn suspects internal problems as the cause of Home Renovations not capturing its share of this growth. However, he is unsure about the problems and their resolution. He has allowed you to buy into the organization in the expectation that you will identify and solve the problems.

You devoted your first month to understanding the organization. The following paragraphs summarize your initial findings.

Homeowners generate renovation business by requesting an estimate for some renovation work. Examples would be a new roof, an external extension, rooms in the basement, and a wooden deck. Mr. Flynn sends an estimator/project manager at the first mutually convenient time. This meeting leads to a written quotation for the renovation, which is usually in competition with other renovators. If the quotation is successful, Mr. Flynn assigns the first available estimator/project manager. That estimator/project manager will hire the trades persons such as plumbers, carpenters, cement makers, insulators, drywallers, and electricians for the various components of the project. The estimator/project manager will order the materials, which he will deliver or arrange for the vendor to deliver to the job.

Estimators/project managers are generally skilled in two trades, plus experienced in estimating projects and managing them to completion. In this dual role,

they estimate the likely cost of renovation projects and manage renovation projects. The dual role ensures high utilization of time. Managing projects is a means of basing estimates on a thorough understanding of actual projects.

Renovation projects average $15,000. The average project requires a lapsed time of 5 weeks from start to completion and three trades persons. Quotations would include a 20 percent markup for overhead and the project manager's time. Thus, the $15,000 job would be $12,500 for trades and materials plus 20 percent or $2,500.

About all the jobs are completed on time, but just as many exceed the cost estimate. When the project manager tries to collect on cost overruns, the customer often is reluctant to pay the extra. Generally only 20 percent of the overruns are collected. The remainder is written off. Last year these overruns reduced the operating income by half. Moreover, the request for additional money creates ill will and reduces repeat business.

You investigated the last 160 jobs, and found that 75 of them had overruns. Of the 75, 70 were where the person who managed the project was not the original estimator. Also, you noticed that all overruns were because of trade costs. There were no material overruns.

As you preceded with the investigation, you asked all estimators/project managers why they had overruns. Their explanations were that the projects were incorrectly estimated. They said the projects could not be completed within the cost estimate. Similarly, you asked each estimator/project manager why others were not able to bring their estimated projects to completion within the cost estimate. Their answers were that the other estimator/project managers did not always expect much from the trades when someone else estimated the project.

You then reviewed the process used for contracting trades. The office staff maintains a list of trades available for work. The system is based on trade type and equality. For each trade there is a list and the listed names are organized according to order of registering. When, for example, a cement maker is needed, the first name is chosen. If that person is not available, the name is placed at the end of the list (after three "unavailable" a name is dropped). If available the trades person is used, and his/her name is placed at the end of the list.

When assigned, the estimator/project manager tells the trades person what must be done and the completion date for key aspects of the project. A trades person usually works on two or three projects at Home Renovations simultaneously. This is necessary to average 20 hours of work or more per week. Weekly hours will vary with the number of active trades persons on the lists.

The monthly financial statements are based on GAAP. Revenues are estimated based on the percentage of completed contracts, less incurred materials, trades, and period expenses which include salaries and wages. The latter includes all 15 employees plus Mr. Flynn and yourself. The accountant calculates the profitability of each project at the end of the year. This helps with reassessing the markup for fixed overhead and profits.

Required Prepare a report to Mr. Flynn analysing the problems at Home Renovations and the recommendations that will resolve them.

Inner Streets Youth Drama Association

Seven years ago, Jean Nadeau formed Inner Streets Youth Drama Association (ISYDA) to help runaway and homeless youth to leave the downtown streets of a large Western Canadian city. These young people have run away from home and dropped out of school. At ages of 12 to 22 they are occupied with alcohol, drugs, petty crime, and prostitution. They are split almost evenly between males and females and about 60 percent have some native background. Most have no regular places to stay at night.

Jean had a similar background, but had managed to leave the streets and get an education, first a bachelor then a master's degree in education. Despite having natural teaching abilities and a very high grade point average, Jean never became a teacher. Instead, he started ISYDA, with little financial support.

ISYDA believes that the problems of street kids are the result of painful experiences and low self-esteem. It also believes that these problems are solvable through self-expression and by taking charge of one's life. Drama is a vehicle for self-expression, and so ISYDA started drama groups in downtown social agencies frequented by the street youth. The youth developed skits and plays depicting their lives and problems. Through discussion among themselves and with audiences, they gained greater understanding of themselves, their families and their friends. ISYDA also started preventative programs in several junior and senior high schools where there were youth at risk of street lives. In these school programs, participants were referred by teachers. Referrals also came from fellow students. Community groups around the province began to request ISYDA plays and workshops and other sessions on how to develop similar drama programs.

ISYDA participants develop the plays themselves, with Jean or other facilitators helping in the process. Their drama concerns included such issues as drugs, prostitution on the streets and AIDS.

ISYDA also has a residential program because participants in the drama programs often have no places to stay. The association rented a large house for sub-lease to the youth. It is for short-term accommodation only and if the young people have social assistance. They pay for rent and food. Jean lives in the house, but the youth make the rules.

By teaching the youth to understand themselves and their situation, drama acted as a means of getting the youth off the streets. This worked in two ways. First, while in the group, they were off the street, at least temporarily. Second, the therapy achieved through drama helped them to resolve many of their problems, and so they became able to pursue off-the-streets alternatives such as attending school, returning home, or obtaining employment. Due to its success in getting a significant number of young people off the streets either temporarily or permanently, ISYDA also became successful at raising funds for operations and capital expenditures.

There are five sources of funds. The first source is foundations that have in their mandates the support of social service activities such as ISYDA. This source supplies start-up or special undertakings such as drama tours or drama camps. There is a limit to the number of years a group receives funding from this type of source. During ISYDA's middle years, it was the most important source of funds.

The second source is ongoing operational funding. This comes from several agencies funded by the government, and this funding signifies an acceptance of the importance and effectiveness of an agency. About two years ago, ISYDA began receiving this funding for about half its operating costs; this is currently its largest source of funding.

The third source is federal and provincial employment grants, at minimum wage rates. This was the most important source of funds in the first few years of ISYDA; then the grants paid Jean and the facilitators. More lately, they pay youth to obtain work skills.

Fourth, performances and workshops generate money. ISYDA, the youth performers, and support staff share this money. Some years, depending on the particular plays and talents of the actors, this has been as much as 20 percent of total revenues.

The last source is donations. This can come from individuals or groups. For example, a local technical college repaired extensively a $1,000, 15-person van for the wholesale cost of parts. A service club denoted the other van. (ISYDA records the market value of donations as revenue.)

ISYDA is a dynamic organization, carrying on a multitude of flexible programs that respond to the youth clients and their circumstances. Each program constitutes an organizational unit or responsibility centre. Each program has a set of definite expectations, e.g., method of operation, number of clients, and client progress by period. It is the organizational formulation of these expectations for helping street youth that entices support from funding agencies.

Jean sees the structure capturing the special attributes of ISYDA, as noted in the chart in Exhibit 1.

ISYDA has been successful both with helping street youth and with raising funds. Exhibit 2 shows the expenditures for the latest year. Jean is the only full-time employee. He hires part-time facilitators and administrators as needed. The focus is on helping the clients and not on a permanent organization. It is crucial to avoid deficits.

Each program has detailed and accurate records as funding agencies require feedback on how their monies were spent and with what results

(i.e., the number of youth helped). The youth are readily identifiable by program, and so is the funding. However, expenditures can be direct or indirect. The direct costs are the hours an employee devotes to a program as a proportion of his or her work day times total remuneration. Other direct costs would include materials, any monies paid to the youth for performances or practices, and snacks. (Provision of snacks has always been a component of programs, as many youth are living in atypical settings. They often come to practices and performances hungry. The snack may include a restaurant meal when on tour — i.e., McDonalds — but most often includes the purchase of food to prepare sandwiches or even a hot meal.)

Indirect costs are more difficult to allocate and some are even joint. Gasoline and other transportation costs are usually difficult to allocate, but the travel record could be used to allocate them to programs. Each travelled kilometre relates to a program.

You have recently joined the board of directors as the (volunteer) treasurer. In the meetings you have had with the board, funding agencies, and Jean, there have been suggestions that there are shortcomings with the accounting information. An executive director of one of the larger funding agencies put the problem succinctly when she said, "We provide ISYDA with money, but we are not sure where the money goes. Sure, for the programs we are funding, we get client numbers and their progress. We appreciate this. However, we would like to know how the money is spent within the programs we fund." ISYDA submits financial statements for the total organization to all funding agencies. Sometimes this pacifies them, but some

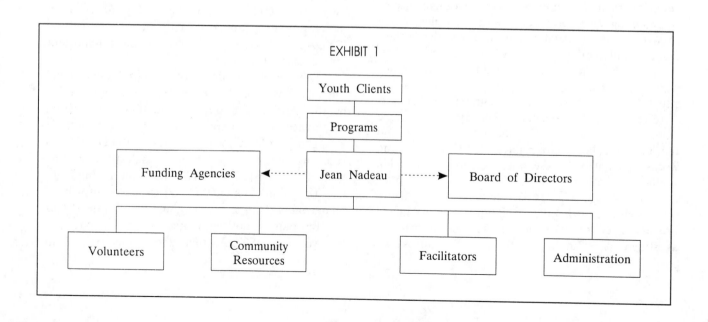

EXHIBIT 1

EXHIBIT 2

INNER STREETS YOUTH DRAMA ASSOCIATION
Income Statement
For the Year Ended December 31, 2001

	2001	2000	1999
REVENUES			
Government funding	$ 60,000	$ —	$ —
Foundation grants	22,000	42,000	21,000
Performance, workshop	10,905	9,652	9,876
Employment grants	7,305	17,854	10,554
Rent	5,400	1,700	—
Donations	6,940	21,893	2,575
Total	112,550	93,099	44,005
EXPENSES			
Salaries, benefits	33,100	30,600	20,000
Contract employee payments	27,500	25,500	9,500
Transportation	24,250	21,200	9,000
Snacks	3,200	2,500	3,500
Rent on house	11,100	4,900	—
House utilities, repairs	3,500	1,900	—
Food at house	4,200	1,500	—
Administration	5,100	4,400	2,300
Total	111,950	92,500	44,300
NET REVENUE	$ 600	$ 599	$ (295)

INNER STREETS YOUTH DRAMA ASSOCIATION
Balance Sheet
As of December 31, 2001

	2001	2000	1999
ASSETS			
Cash	$10,050	$ 5,000	$ 1,000
Accounts receivable	9,450	10,000	8,000
Inventory, supplies	150	100	50
Prepaid rent	900	900	—
Fixed assets, vehicles, net	20,500	15,500	1,000
Total	$41,050	$31,500	$10,050
LIABILITIES			
Accounts payable	$ 1,500	$ 2,000	$ 1,000
Unearned revenue	38,146	28,696	8,845
SURPLUS (DEFICIT)			
Accrued to current year	804	205	500
For 1992	600	599	(295)
Total	$41,050	$31,500	$10,050

request more specific information, which requires hurried projects for allocating costs to individual programs or sub-programs.

With this concern in mind, you review the accounting system with Jean and a volunteer who inputs the financial transaction data with a computer accounting package. The accounting format is for a single entity. Nevertheless, the package being used has the capacity to report revenues and expenses for 10 programs plus consolidating. Exhibit 2 shows the financial statements for ISYDA.

You note that there are nine different programs as shown below:

- Riverbend Community Centre
- J.J. Laurier Drop-in Shelter
- Southwest High School
- Southwest Junior High School
- Crump Junior and Senior High School
- Northern Tour
- Central Tour
- Summer Camp
- House

Required The board of directors asked you to address the concerns of the funding agencies for regularly produced accounting information by program. Be specific regarding individual expenditures and accounting practices.

CASE 14

Jones Company

Edward Jones started the Jones Company Limited (JCL) as a sole proprietorship. It was later incorporated; ownership is now 50 percent controlled by Mr. Jones, who is 71 years old, and 25 percent each by his sons, John and Carl.

JCL started 30 years ago with a single lumberyard in Sleepyside. Edward later expanded into nearby towns and recently two more lumberyards were added — another in Sleepyside. Currently, there are eight lumberyards selling lumber and building materials. Approximately 85 percent of the sales are to retail customers while the remaining sales go to approximately 75 contractors.

John Jones went to work for his father's lumberyard business directly after high school. In 15 years, he worked hard in almost all positions in the business, and became knowledgeable, liked, and respected by essentially all employees. Five years ago, John received the title of general manager of the lumberyard division.

Carl Jones, after studying mechanical engineering at a university, worked for four years with a firm of consulting engineers located in another city. Six years ago, Edward established a separate division of JCL that manufactures construction lumber. Because he wanted both of his sons to be involved in the family business, Edward offered to Carl the position of general manager of this newly established manufacturing division. Carl immediately accepted. Initially, this division produced lumber only for JCL's lumberyard; however, after four years, the manufacturing division expanded and started selling to wholesalers and other retailers.

Recent Events

In recent months, Edward Jones has begun to realize that management at JCL requires some changes to improve efficiency and effectiveness. His first impression is that control needs improvement, but he is aware of his own bias, and thus, admits the problems may be more extensive than he recognizes. Specific recent events have influenced him. For one, suppliers, employees, and customers have been complaining that it takes too long for JCL and its divisions to "get things done." Dissatisfied customers say JCL has become too big for the old way of management.

There have also been suggestions that the president's large workload leads to bottlenecks. Employees have levelled increasing criticism at the organization's reporting structure. Exhibit 1 shows the president's version of the organization structure.

In the past year, some long-term customers have stopped dealing with the lumberyard division and have taken their contractor requirements to other dealers. The most common explanation given by the customers upon moving their business is that JCL cannot guarantee delivery dates.

There has been substantial and constant disagreement on the transfer price at which the manufacturing division sells to the lumberyard division. It is uncertain whether this is the cause of the lumberyard division's declining profitability or whether geographical expansion is to blame. There is concern about the manufacturing division's financial profitability. The organization's profitability is difficult to verify because of the substantial sales made to the lumberyard division at a different price than market.

The manufacturing division is unsure if its primary purpose is to provide lumber to the lumberyard division, or to operate as an independent profit centre that also sells to a sister division. Similarly, the lumberyard division is unsure if its primary purpose is to provide a retail outlet for the manufacturing division's output or to maximize its profit potential as a lumber and building materials retailer and contractor supplier.

Unexpectedly, a Sleepyside developer offered to purchase the land that the main Sleepyside lumberyard occupies, and to relocate the lumberyard to another comparable site. In exchange for the present site, the developer has offered to provide a larger lot in another part of town, to build a comparable store, move all shelving, racking and

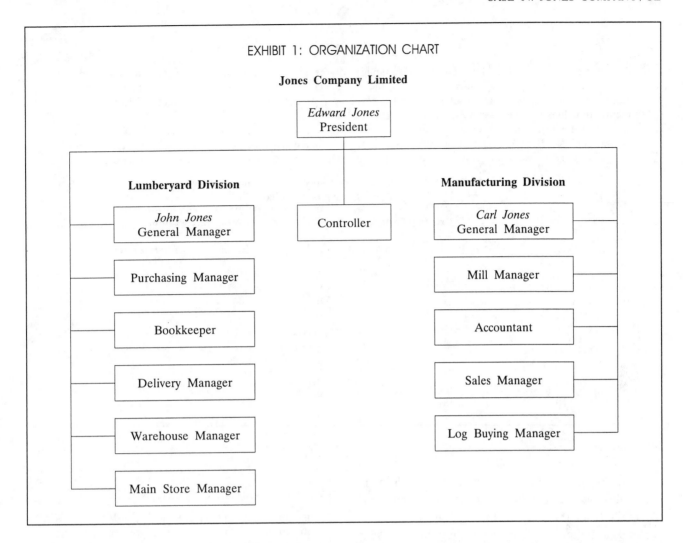

EXHIBIT 1: ORGANIZATION CHART

Jones Company Limited

Edward Jones
President

Lumberyard Division

John Jones
General Manager

Purchasing Manager

Bookkeeper

Delivery Manager

Warehouse Manager

Main Store Manager

Controller

Manufacturing Division

Carl Jones
General Manager

Mill Manager

Accountant

Sales Manager

Log Buying Manager

inventory to the new facility, and pay $5 million. Exhibit 2 shows the estimated net income and amortization for each site. The offer has been outstanding for eight months; the developer wants an acceptance within a month or it will be withdrawn.

Some of these problems have been festering for years. Many have become aggravated to such an extent that something must be done soon to preserve the viability of JCL.

The New Corporate Controller

To obtain better control, JCL has hired you as the corporate controller, reporting to the president. Your duties include developing, implementing, and administering financial reporting and budgeting systems. Also, you are the treasurer.

During your first week, you discussed some high priority projects with the president. For one, the president wants an assessment of the financial reporting and budgeting systems, and recommendations for improvements. As part of his concern

with reporting, the president wonders if the present organization structure is appropriate and where responsibilities for financial reporting and budgeting should be placed.

You and the president had lunch with one of his friends who had enthusiastically explained the advantages of strategic planning for improving a firm's performance. You had concurred with the opinion that strategic planning would be beneficial to JCL. In private, you told the president that you would later explain the advantages of strategic planning for JCL. The president believes strategic planning can help with the current problems.

There are two specific requirements that the president also wants you to address. You have been asked:

• To determine whether the developer's offer to swap land is sufficiently attractive to accept. Exhibit 2 describes the offer. (The president said the company's cost of capital is approximately 15%.)

EXHIBIT 2: LAND SWAP

At the request of the president, the general manager of the lumberyard division calculated the expected net income (after all cash and non-cash expenses, including income taxes) for both the existing main Sleepyside store and the proposed facility offered by the developer. Amortization schedules reflect differences in the recorded values of the respective old and new buildings.

The developer had agreed to pay JCL $5 million up front. This payment would result in a $2.5 million capital gain for JCL. At the end of 10 years, the general manager expects that there will not be any significant difference between the two alternatives in terms of net income, amortization, assets, and land values.

Comparison Between Two Locations for the Main Sleepyside Store
(in thousands of dollars)

	Existing Facility		Proposed Facility	
Year	Net Income	Amortization	Net Income	Amortization
1	$1,000	$50	$ 700	$70
2	1,070	50	777	70
3	1,144	50	862	70
4	1,225	50	957	70
5	1,311	50	1,063	70
6	1,403	50	1,180	70
7	1,501	50	1,309	70
8	1,606	50	1,453	70
9	1,718	50	1,613	70
10	1,838	50	1,800	70

• To determine what the lumberyard division would have paid under market conditions for lumber from the manufacturing division. Recommend a better method for setting the transfer price, if one exists.

You want to address JCL's current difficulties within your first month at your new job. You decided to spend a week interviewing all persons reporting to the president and reviewing relevant documents. Exhibit 3 shows the guide you used to conduct the interviews. The document review included all relevant studies, statistics, financial statements, and operating reports.

Performance, Reporting and Budgeting

With your interviews and document reviews, you gained a better appreciation of JCL and its divisions.

Many managers said that the firm does not have a clear understanding of where it is going with its divisions, and consequently, decision making is difficult.

In recent years, profits of the divisions have declined, as noted in the tables of Exhibit 4. For the lumberyard division, the decline persisted after adjustment for changes in sales mix. That is, the

EXHIBIT 3: INTERVIEW GUIDE

In conducting interviews with persons at JCL who report to the president, you as the corporate controller established an interview guide to ensure consistency and thoroughness. The guide contained the following questions:

1. What are the responsibilities and authorities of your position?

2. What are the perceived objectives of your position?

3. What relationships do you have with other managers in your division and with managers in the other division?

4. How reliable and useful are the accounting records?

5. How are activities planned, budgeted, monitored, and evaluated?

6. How available are data on the quality and cost-effectiveness of work performed?

division increased the proportion of its sales going to high profit, non-lumber merchandise after 1997.

There is general agreement among managers that the financial reports are reliable, timely, and accurate in reporting revenue and expense items.

EXHIBIT 4: PROFITABILITY

Lumberyard Profitability

	Return on Investment (%)			Return on Sales (%)		
	Actual	Adjusted	Industry	Actual	Adjusted	Industry
1992	14.8	14.8	14.2	6.8	6.8	7.1
1993	14.2	14.2	13.8	7.1	7.1	6.9
1994	13.8	13.8	13.0	6.9	6.9	6.5
1995	13.0	13.0	13.4	6.5	6.5	6.7
1996	12.8	12.8	14.2	6.4	6.4	7.1
1997	13.2	13.2	14.0	6.6	6.6	7.0
1998	10.8	10.6	13.2	6.0	5.9	6.6
1999	9.7	9.2	13.4	5.4	5.1	6.7
2000	8.8	8.5	14.4	5.2	5.0	7.2
2001	9.1	8.6	13.6	5.1	4.9	6.8

Manufacturing Profitability

	Return on Investment (%)		Return on Sales (%)	
	Division	Industry	Division	Industry
1998	6.4	24.0	4.0	15.0
1999	12.8	23.7	8.0	14.8
2000	15.8	22.0	9.5	13.8
2001	17.3	24.3	10.8	15.2

Three reports are prepared monthly: a profit and loss statement for each division and one for JCL. The balance sheets and statements of sources and applications of funds are prepared annually by an outside accountant. Financial statements for 2001 are presented in Exhibits 5, 6, and 7.

The commitment accounting system in use by both divisions is particularly useful in keeping expenditures within budget because it recognizes committed expenses when purchase orders are placed. As well, on the profit and loss statement, a separate column records committed amounts. The total of commitments and expenditures determines what is left of a budget. Payment of an invoice cancels its commitment.

The manufacturing division's direct costing system is simple and well understood. The mill manager has asked whether he should record "down time" and "paid but not worked time" as suggested by an article he read. Currently, the coding does not separately identify these items.

The annual budgets are concerned with expenditure control. One manager glibly said "I could stay within the budget and achieve nothing. No one would know or care." Performance is measured by sales. Managers were vague when asked about objectives, performance measures and priorities. JCL's managers do not complete their budgets until late March, nearly three months after the start of the new year.

The president approves all purchase orders of more than $200 and the hiring of all employees. This has led to the hoarding of inventory and employees, and has reduced the flexibility with which each division can alter these resources. Moreover, the president often initiates or approves expenditures. He thus bypasses the budgetary process and the general managers who are responsible for achieving the budgets.

There is a duplication of responsibilities between the president and the general managers. Profitability is the responsibility of the respective general manager. However, many divisional employees report to the president, or in other cases, there is confusion over reporting relationships. In addition, the president makes many decisions that the general managers think they should make, e.g., vacation schedules. There are personality problems in each division, detracting from smooth operations. A typical example is that three times the manufacturing mill shut down due to a lack of logs; conflict between the manufacturing

EXHIBIT 5

JONES COMPANY LIMITED
— LUMBERYARD DIVISION
Profit and Loss Statement
For the Year Ending December 31, 2001
(in thousands of dollars)

Net sales	$12,000
Cost of goods sold	7,200
Merchandise gross profit	4,800
Additional income:	
Interest income	120
Bad debts recovered	50
Delivery income	170
Contracting income	60
Miscellaneous income	210
Total additional income	610
Gross profit	5,410
Expenses:	
Salaries and wages	2,100
Truck and auto expenses	400
Amortization	300
Bad debts	118
Utilities	250
Rent	500
Miscellaneous	614
Total expenses	4,282
Net profit before taxes	1,128
Provision for income taxes	519
Net Profit	$ 609

Balance Sheet
As at December 31, 2001
(in thousands of dollars)

Working capital	$ 5,600
Fixed assets	1,050
	6,650
Less: Long-term debt	5,700
Investment	$ 950

EXHIBIT 6

JONES COMPANY LIMITED
— MANUFACTURING DIVISION
Profit and Loss Statement
For the Year Ending December 31, 2001
(in thousands of dollars)

Net sales	$14,000
Cost of goods sold	7,250
Gross margin	6,750
Other income	135
Gross profit	6,885
Expenses:	
Indirect manufacturing costs	2,170
Sales	875
Administration	1,040
Total expenses	4,085
Net profits before taxes	2,800
Provision for income taxes	1,288
Net profit	$ 1,512

Balance Sheet
As at December 31, 2001
(in thousands of dollars)

Working capital	$ 2,625
Fixed assets	6,125
	8,750
Less: Long-term debt	600
Investment	$ 8,150

division's purchasing manager and its mill manager caused the shutdown.

The president has the heaviest workload of all managers. With JCL's growth, this workload means that those things that once were done immediately now take days to complete. This lag delays purchase order approvals. Managers below the level of general manager are unhappy with the limited scope allowed them in carrying out their responsibilities. The result is a higher rate of turnover among managers in the lumber division than that experienced by competitors; the comparison data comes from the Retail Lumber Dealers Association. Moreover, the high rate demands consider-

able employee and management time devoted to recruitment and training of replacements.

There are frequent quality and quantity differences between what the lumberyard division ordered from the manufacturing division and what it received. Moreover, the timing of shipments is unpredictable. Because of these difficulties, the lumberyard division has at times had to purchase lumber at higher prices from competitors in situations in order to meet delivery commitments.

There is a lack of regularly reported information (e.g., sales per salesperson, deliveries per driver, labour hours per thousand board feet, etc.) pertaining to efficiency and effectiveness.

The manufacturing division sells lumber to the lumberyard division for direct cost plus a 25 percent markup. On average, this transfer price is higher than the market, and has become increasingly higher during the last two years. A telephone interview with the executive director of the provincial Retail Lumber Dealers Association confirmed the lumberyard division general manager's allegation that the pricing of large long-term contracts is at a discount from the spot market, usually 5 percent. The following table shows these details:

Lumber Transferred, Manufacturing to Lumberyard Division

	Boardfeet (000s)	Direct Manufacturing Costs (000s)	Market Price* Boardfeet (000s)
1998	11.67	$2,625	$336
1999	12.04	3,010	291
2000	11.27	3,100	310
2001	12.00	3,600	326

* Weighted to reflect the different grades and lengths of lumber transferred.

"Sales turnover" (sales / assets) for the lumberyard division has changed in recent years. A survey has shown that competitors have also experienced a change in sales turnover during the same years. The table below shows the patterns:

Lumberyard Sales Turnover

	Division	Competition
1992	2.47	2.43
1993	2.51	2.53
1994	2.34	2.49
1995	2.30	2.55
1996	2.36	2.61
1997	1.98	2.64
1998	1.96	2.71
1999	1.90	2.81
2000	1.95	2.77
2001	1.81	2.73

The main lumberyard in Sleepyside had recently entered the contracting business. The profitability of these ventures has been minimal. Profits would have been even less had Reg Smith, the main Sleepyside store manager and JCL's first employee, applied the standard contractor discount of 20 percent to lumber sold to the ventures. Lower costs made some projects profitable.

The sales to contractors by the lumberyard division have decreased as a percent of total sales and in constant dollar terms during the last five years. However, retail sales have been growing at a faster rate than the industry average. Manufacturing division sales have also been growing at a more rapid rate than experienced by the industry. This is a result of lumber quality and sales penetration of new markets.

In the manufacturing division, the sales department frequently initiates special orders of lumber. The mill manager claims that these orders are

---

EXHIBIT 7

JONES COMPANY LIMITED
Profit and Loss Statement
For the Year Ending December 31, 2001
(in thousands of dollars)

Net Sales	$21,500
Cost of goods sold	9,950
Gross margin	11,550
Additional income	745
Gross profit	12,295
Total expenses	8,367
Net profit before taxes	3,928
Provision for income taxes	1,807
Net Profit	$ 2,121

Balance Sheet
As at December 31, 2001
(in thousands of dollars)

Working capital	$ 8,225
Fixed assets	7,175
	15,400
Less: Long-term debt	6,300
Total shareholders' equity	$ 9,100

Statement of Sources and Application of Funds
For the Year Ending December 31, 2001
(in thousands of dollars)

SOURCES	
Operations	$ 2,067
Non-cash expenditures	810
	2,877
Issue debt	5,375
Total sources	$ 8,252
APPLICATIONS	
Purchase equipment	$ 2,705
Pay dividends	205
Redeem capital stock	4,000
Add to working capital	1,342
Total applications	$ 8,252

---

more expensive than regular production and has repeatedly asked for recognition of this in pricing.

Required You, as the corporate controller, must prepare a concise, well-written report to the president of your investigation in which you highlight and analyse those areas of JCL that need management attention. Your report should include practical recommendations for management action.

CASE 15

King Coal

The provincial government's electrical utility has a coal mine in the King region that produces thermal and metallurgical coal using an integrated pit mine and cleaning plant. Separate reporting is not done for the extraction and cleaning plant or for the thermal coal and metallurgical coal. The assumption is that if the total cost is competitive then each part must be efficient. Although this may have been a reasonable approximation in the past, new mines have been opened that are more efficient. Now the utility's senior management wants to manage the cost of each part individually.

The controller has assigned you to calculate the profitability of the operations. The reason for your assignment is to figure out, as accurately as possible, the exact costs of each coal and each operation at the King Mine. Then you are to compare the costs with other operations of the utility and with industry averages. These costs will be the starting points for specifying annual improvements in productivity and cost-effectiveness. A component of this study will be to devise a transfer price between the extraction and cleaning plant, if that would motivate cost-effectiveness. When he assigned the project, the controller conveyed the transfer price idea of a board member, but admitted he does not understand why it would be beneficial. The controller asks that you explain transfer pricing and its possible benefits in your report.

EXHIBIT 1

KING MINE DIVISION
Operating Statement
For the Year Ending December 31, 2001
(in thousands of dollars)

REVENUE		
Thermal coal		$ —
Metallurgical coal		11,700
EXPENSES		
Extraction wages and benefits	$10,500	
Plant wages and benefits	9,500	
Diesel fuel, gasoline	3,800	
Amortization, pit trucks, equipment*	3,000	
Amortization, busses*	900	
Amortization, plant equipment*	2,800	
Amortization, costs	800	
Management salaries and benefits	2,700	
Administration	2,300	
Facilities, utilities and taxes	2,600	
Marketing department	800	39,700
Net income before income taxes		$(28,000)

* Amortization is based on the physical exhaustion of the asset

---

The production process includes the extraction and hauling of raw coal to the cleaning plant. The cleaning plant prepares both types of coal for shipment by rail, the thermal to a thermal plant and the metallurgical to a private steel mill.

The financial performances of the extraction and cleaning operations, and the ancillary support and administrative activities combine into a single operating statement. The statement is shown in Exhibit 1. You realize that to accomplish your project you will need to allocate these costs to the two coals and two operations. Subsequently, you arrange appointments with managers and other employees who are knowledgeable concerning the content and drivers for each expense line item.

Employees travel by company bus from two towns where they live to the mine site. The last twenty-seven kilometres into the mine is a company-maintained road.

You find that the annual contract for thermal coal is 450,000 tonnes and 150,000 tonnes for metallurgical coal. For each contract, King mine is the prime supplier and the customers make up any shortage by alternative and more expensive secondary suppliers. The mine ships the full amount for contract each year. The metallurgical coal generates revenue at the rate of $78 per tonne. The thermal coal does not generate revenue because it is shipped to a thermal plant owned by provincial government. To estimate a transfer price, you ask the general manager for the thermal plant what would be the landed cost of thermal coal on a long-term contract. She estimated the cost to be $71 per tonne (delivered) for comparable coal. The traffic officer (responsible for arranging for and monitoring transportation) explained that King ships clean coal at the cost of $6 a tonne.

The mine is a series of interlinked pit mines that produce 652,000 tonnes per year. Excavation equipment and trucks remove the overburden. The pits differ by coal type, and for efficiency purposes the miners extract thermal coal for three weeks, and then metallurgical coal in the fourth. Pit mining wages and benefits, amortization for pit trucks and equipment, and depletion costs are entirely attributable to the extraction of the coal. These costs are the same per tonne for both thermal and metallurgical coal.

Shrinkage in the cleaning plant through the elimination of impurities reduces the weight by 8 percent. The expenses for the cleaning plant include plant wages and benefits and amortization for plant and equipment. The metallurgical process has additional stages and thus a higher cost per tonne than thermal coal. You estimate 70 percent of all cleaning costs are attributable to thermal coal and 30 percent to metallurgical coal.

Diesel fuel and gasoline expenses track to tank locations and invoiced prices. You estimate that $3,500,000 was for extraction, $150,000 was for the loaders in the plant, and $150,000 was for the buses.

There are nine buses scheduled to drive back and forth between the two towns and the mine site where all employees report for work; 500,000 kilometres were driven last year. Employees take the bus about 98 percent of the time. The following table shows the breakdown of employees by department:

Extraction	41%
Plant	26
Management	13
Administration	15
Marketing	5

When analysed according to where they work or how they devote their average work day, the management, administration, and marketing personnel had the following to say in aggregate:

	Extraction	Plant	Neither	Total
Management	45	35	20	100%
Administration	45	40	15	100%
Marketing	—	—	100	100%

About $600,000 of the administration expense item is attributable to buses. Square feet occupied is the cost driver for facilities, utilities and municipal taxes. You calculate the allocation to be 45 percent for extraction, 35 percent for plant, 10 percent for administration, 5 percent for management, and 5 percent for marketing.

Required   Complete your assignment.

Major Electronics

Major Electronics is a multi-plant assembler of computers and computer products. It has 40 plants located in southern Ontario and greater Montreal. In recent years, there have been concerns that its traditional method for allocating manufacturing overhead (MOH) is no longer relevant. Direct labour costs now average 6 percent of manufacturing costs for its 40 plants, with 55 percent for direct materials, and 39 percent for manufacturing overhead.

The corporate management accounting branch is investigating alternative cost drivers. MOH is divided into three groups: procurement, production, and support. The standard chart of accounts for Major further classifies these costs into sub-classes (see Exhibit 1), which are ranked in order of importance.

The corporate management accounting branch surveyed manufacturing managers at all 40 plants to obtain a list of the most important cost drivers for MOH. With these cost drivers, an analysis was done to ascertain their correlation coefficient (r)

with MOH in total and each of the three major groups. Each r is shown in Exhibit 2.

These results were presented to a group of plant managers that was formed to provide advice to the corporate management accounting branch on the development of alternative cost drivers. The committee was not surprised at the correlations. However they had two concerns that could not be immediately resolved. First, the committee was unclear about how a positive r in regression analysis implied the respective costs were driven by a cost driver. With regression analysis, there is a constant (or alpha or intercept) and a slope (or beta). The slope coefficient is comparable to variable costs per unit of the cost driver. The constant is comparable to the fixed costs, but beyond the relevant range. Many members of the advisory group were puzzled about whether total indirect costs from a pool should be allocated, or just the variable costs? Second, some overhead costs have been incurred for capacities much greater than current production. For example, in most plants the

---

EXHIBIT 1: SUB-CLASSIFICATION OF MANUFACTURING OVERHEAD COSTS

Procurement	Production	Support
• Stores	• Direct labour payroll taxes and benefits	• Production engineering
• Purchasing	• Occupancy	• Process engineering
• Materials	• Direct labour supervision	• Manufacturing management
• engineering	• Other indirect labour	• Quality assurance
• Materials management	• Operating expenses	
• Production control	• Amortization	
• Material specification	• Production management	
• Inbound freight	• Equipment expenses	
• Traffic and receiving	• Shipping	
• Corporate materials charges		

EXHIBIT 2

Cost Driver	Total MOH	Procurement	Production	Support
Total manufacturing space	0.57	0.32	0.50	0.49
Average total head-count in manufacturing	0.86	0.44	0.81	0.56
Direct labour dollars	0.73	0.12	0.77	0.45
Direct material dollars	0.17	−0.12	−0.44	−0.30
Number of part numbers	0.13	0.45	0.16	−0.06
Percent of parts inspected on receipt	0.00	0.24	−0.11	0.16
Number of products	0.53	0.19	0.50	0.59
Number of customer orders per month	−0.05	−0.04	−0.07	0.08
Average cycle time in days	0.10	−0.21	0.19	0.21

materials specifications units operate at 50 percent of their full capacity. Many members thought underutilized capacity should not be allocated to existing products. It was thought that this would not be fair when facing competitors that were operating at full capacity.

Required As the project manager for the alternative cost drivers project, prepare a report using the case approach that makes recommendations for a successful project.

McKenzies Department Stores

Your family entered the Canadian retail business in 1869. Your great, great grandfather operated a general store in Newmarket, Ontario from 1869 to 1875, and then moved to Toronto where he bought dry goods and haberdashery businesses located at the intersection of King and Yonge Streets. He was one of the first Canadian merchants to sell goods at visibly marked prices for cash. Before this retail innovation, merchandise was sold on credit at negotiable prices. Marked, cash prices turned out to be a competitive advantage to your great, great grandfather who expanded in store size and by product lines. By 1912 McKenzies was the largest department store chain in Canada, with a catalogue division that supplied merchandise to rural customers not within easy access to any of its urban department stores.

Then in 1935, with the department stores catering to middle and high income customers, McKenzies was augmented by the acquisition of a chain of junior department stores that appealed to the more budget-minded. In addition to the two largely different sets of merchandise, the regular department stores had larger gross margins (revenue less cost of goods sold divided by revenue) and lower turnovers (revenue divided by inventory) compared to the junior department stores or discount stores which had smaller gross margins and higher turnovers.

In the late 1950s and early 1960s, McKenzies followed population migration by establishing department stores in suburban malls. By the 1980s McKenzies was meeting the challenges of new discount store competitors by expanding and refocusing its junior department store chain, re-named Bargos. Threats came from Wal-Mart in the 1990s. Now, the threat seems to be coming from Internet retailers.

Margins and Turnovers

Another way to examine the history of McKenzies is through a study of margins and turnovers. Retailing was dominated during most of the 19th century by local merchants who provided value to their customers by keeping large inventories, extending credit, and offering personalized advice. The merchants' high-inventory, service-intensive business model resulted in slow turnover. Many of these retailers struggled to turn their inventories over twice a year. As a consequence of a high-cost structure, these retailers were forced to charge high prices to earn the margins necessary to stay in business.

The industry changed dramatically in the late 19th century and early 20th century as a result of the first retailing disruption: the launch of department stores. These stores tended to underperform the existing retailers in many aspects of customer service but their other qualities gave them advantages. In particular, they did a superior job of getting their products into the right place. They brought together in one location an enormous number of different goods, making it much easier for shoppers to find what they needed. In effect, the department stores served as the portals of their day; customers knew that if they walked into a good department store they were likely to find what they wanted. The aggregation of customers and products enabled department stores to outperform local stores in pricing. By accelerating inventory turnover rates, they could earn the same returns on much lower gross margins.

Department stores also found a way to mitigate their disadvantage in customer service. As their clerks could not be as knowledgeable about individual customer's needs and preferences as local speciality shop owners, department stores initially tended to focus their merchandise mix on simple, familiar products. Then, as customers grew accustomed to the new format, the department stores introduced more complex products at higher profit margins. This transition to complicated, high profit products was possible when the brand of the retailer became a surrogate for product reliability.

The flourishing of department stores can be traced to a new technology at that time — the railroad. With an infrastructure of railroads in place, department stores could aggregate goods from all over the country. At the same time, rail trolleys could transport customers at the fringes of town to the urban-centre department stores. Thus, site location became a source of competitive advantage and to be managed scientifically. For example, department store chains hired "traffic counters" to tabulate the number of potential customers walking past busy street corners.

At the same time that department stores were springing up in cities, another very different disruption was also taking place — catalogue retailing. Originally targeted at rural customers who could not easily visit department stores, mail-order catalogues were made possible by the introduction of rural free mail delivery. One department store chain touted its catalogue as "the cheapest supply house on earth" and it compensated for the lack of personal service with money-back guarantees. Catalogues were, in essence, an early equivalent of today's virtual department stores.

Another technological advance — the automobile — set in motion the next retailing revolution. First, the automobile made shopping malls possible. Although malls proved a real threat to department stores, they did not alter the fundamental business model. They were a sustaining innovation, not a disruptive one. Malls did the same thing that department stores did, only better. They attracted enough customers to enable a collection of focused retailers to achieve similar margins and inventory turns as department stores, but with deeper product lines within each category. For the first three decades after shopping malls appeared, department stores continued to play crucial roles as anchors, using their strong brands to draw shoppers. By making shoppers comfortable with malls, the department stores contributed to their own obsolescence. Specifically, many present-day strip and outlet malls are simply aggregations of category-focused retailers, which thrive in the absence of department stores.

A similar transformation took place in catalogue retailing. As customers became accustomed to making purchases through the mail, hundreds of specialty catalogues appeared. They chipped away at the sales of the generalist catalogues of department stores. The automobile also made a second wave of innovation possible: the establishment of the discount department stores in the early 1960s. The increased mobility of shoppers enabled discounters to establish outlets at the edge of cities where real estate costs were substantially lower, effectively voiding department stores' competitive advantage with prime locations in city centres.

Unlike malls, discount stores were a disruptive innovation. They made money through a completely different business model that enabled successful discounters to achieve six inventory turns a year with gross margins of about 20 percent. The average successful department earned gross margins of approximately 40 percent and turned its inventory three times for a similar 120 percent annual return on capital invested in inventory.

Discounters initially concentrated on simple products that could sell themselves (as department stores had done earlier). About 80 percent of the floor area of the leading discount stores during the 1960s and 1970s was devoted to branded hard goods such as hardware, kitchen utensils, books, luggage, and packaged personal care products. As the key attributes of such merchandise could be communicated easily — by pictures on the package, the brand of the manufacturer, and a few numbers — the discounters were able to spend even less on customer service than the department stores did.

As the discounters invaded the low ground, the department stores systematically closed down their hard-goods departments and moved upmarket. They became retailers of soft goods such as clothing, home furnishings, and cosmetics — products whose key attributes are more complex and more difficult to communicate. With soft goods being more difficult to sell in the low-service, discount format, department stores were able to maintain the higher margins required to sustain their business model.

During their early years, the discounters were very successful. As long as they priced their goods below the prices of department stores, they could make money. But when the discounters had driven the department stores from the lower tiers of the market, they were competing only against equally low-cost discounters. That competition drove pricing and profits in the branded hard-goods tiers of the market to subsistence levels.

Then a new set of highly focused retailers attacked the discounters. Specialty discounters such as Home Depot and Business Depot carved up the hard-goods market. Like the malls, these category killers represented a sustaining innovation rather than a disruptive one. They offered broader, deeper selections of products within their narrower categories, but they still had the volume to achieve the inventory turns required in the discounters' 20 percent gross-margin times six inventory-turns profit model.

A few discounters, Wal-Mart most notably, have been able to use their purchasing clout and logistics-management capabilities to continue to compete in hard goods. But most of the surviving discount stores have followed the earlier path of the department stores: they have fled the hard-goods competition by migrating upmarket. Indeed, discounters have flipped their original merchandise mix; 60 to 80 percent of their floor space is now devoted to soft goods.

A fourth retailing disruption is now being instigated by the Internet; it promises to alter the retailing landscape as fundamentally as the three earlier disruptions. Of the four dimensions of the retailer's mission — product, place, price, and time — Internet retailers can deliver on the first three remarkably well. The right products? In categories ranging from books to chemicals, Web stores can offer selections that no bricks-and-mortar outlet can match. The right price? Internet retailers enjoy unparalleled margin flexibility. To earn 120 percent profit on inventory investment, an Internet retailer such as Amazon.com, which can turn its inventory 25 times each year, needs only about a 5 percent gross margin. And, the right place? It is here — location — that the Internet is most revolutionary. The Internet negates the importance of location. Anyone, at any time, can become a global retailer by setting up a Web page.

With such advantages, it is no wonder electronic commerce is attracting so much attention. But how should we expect this revolution to occur? As we have seen, there are two clear patterns in the way the earlier retailing disruptions unfolded. First, generalist stores and catalogues dominated retailing at the outset of the disruptions, but they were eventually supplemented by specialized retailers. The specialists emerged once the market for the new form of retailing had grown large enough in sales volume for a narrower but deeper product mix. Second, the disruptive retailers weighted their initial merchandise mix toward products that could sell themselves — simple, branded products whose key attributes could be comprehended visually and numerically. They then shifted their merchandise towards higher-margin, more complex products to maintain their profits in the face of intense competition at the low end of their businesses.

There appears to be a repeat of the early stages of both those patterns in Internet retailing. Leading Internet retailers like Amazon.com have rapidly migrated toward the department store strategy. The logic is clear. The Web is a vast and confusing place, and it is currently very difficult to know who is selling what. Anyone with a few thousand dollars can set up a Web-based business, just as almost anyone with a little money in the 1860s could set up a small shop. The best Internet search engines today can locate only a fraction of the Web sites that exist in a category, and they

are frustratingly inaccurate. Moreover, with such intense advertising noise about us, it is next to impossible to remember which dot-com name is associated with which product or service. Hence, Amazon.com seems to sense the same opportunity that department stores saw. If you need to find a product, you only need to remember how to type "Amazon.com" — or better yet, click on its bookmark — and you will be guided to whatever you need.

It is less clear, though, whether this pattern will unfold as it did in the past. Even the largest bricks-and-mortar department stores could stock only the items with the highest turnover rates within each product category. That limitation opened the door for the specialists. Internet department stores face no such physical limits. They can, in theory, offer the depth of the specialist with the breadth of the generalists.

Perhaps Internet department stores will not yield market share to specialist retailers as the volume of purchases in individual categories grows. But there is a countervailing force. The inevitable emergence of better search engines, together with the availability of greater bandwidth into homes, will make it increasingly easy for consumers to find specialized "e-tailers." The future of Internet department stores and category-focused retailers could be based on the patterns of the past, but the future simply cannot be known at this point. The technologic and economic factors that drove the historical patterns are different in this wave. The pattern will play out: the managerial benefits of focus and the ultimate ease of travel across Web sites will probably give a slight edge, eventually, to focused players. The odds will tilt towards specialists even more if cybermalls emerge that rent space to a collection of specialist retailers whose category brands are strong — akin to the way today's physical shopping malls have evolved.

As with the earlier disruption, Internet retailing has initially focused on the simple end of the merchandise spectrum — books, CDs, publically traded stocks, personal care products., commodity chemicals, etc. The question is, how fast will the disruptions move upmarket into more complex products and value added services?

Already we see signs of upmarket migration. The transformation of some Internet-based retailers into "clicks and mortar" retailers — establishing warehouses and physical stores to give customers faster access to inventory and to handle returns and service issues conveniently and personally — is not an admission that the Internet-retailing model does not work. Rather, just as we saw with department stores years ago, it is a perfectly predictable

EXHIBIT 1: SEGMENTED STATEMENTS OF EARNINGS

(Millions of dollars)

	McKenzies	Bargos	Total*
Sales and revenue	2,594	4,598	7,192
Cost of goods sold	1,556	3,678	5,234
Gross margin	1,038	920	1,958
Operating costs	910	770	1,680
Earnings before interest, taxes	128	150	278
Interest expenses			79
Income taxes			96
Net earnings			103
Number of stores	98	327	
Gross Space, 000s sq. ft.	16,883	28,288	

* Note: The total also includes corporate costs and revenues, plus adjustments.

step. As competition in the simplest tiers heats up, to maintain profitability good managers migrate toward product lines with higher profit margins that accompany value-added services.

The upmarket migration is likely to happen much more rapidly with this wave than it did in the earlier disruptive waves. Traditional retailers have always had to make a trade-off between the richness of information they could exchange with customers and the number of customers they could reach. Although local merchants could exchange rich information about products, the economics of providing such expertise means that they could cater to only a narrow set of customers. To reach a mass market, department stores could not afford to employ expert staff to sell a broad range of complex products. In contrast, the Internet seems capable of breaking this trade-off. It can enable retailers to communicate rich information about a broad set of complex products to a very large set of customers. That capability should help Internet retailers move upmarket more quickly than their forefathers did.

Of course, some products are less suited to electronic sales than others. While Internet retailers excel at getting the right products in the right place at the right price, they are at a disadvantage when it comes to delivering physical products at the right time. When shoppers need products immediately, they will head for their cars, not their computers. There are also certain experiences that the Internet cannot deliver. Even with substantial bandwidth, communicating the feel of clothing and home furnishings will be difficult.

Moreover, in those customer segments where the social experience of shopping is an important element of value, the home-bound nature of on-line commerce offers little appeal.

McKenzies' Anticipated Strategy

After more than a century in retailing, McKenzies has two dominant chains: the department stores (called McKenzies) and the discount stores (called Bargos). (See Exhibit 1 for financial and market presence details.) With over 98 locations across Canada, McKenzies is predominantly a full-line department store chain concentrating on fashion merchandise in apparel, cosmetics, accessories and soft home categories. It offers quality merchandise at mid-to-upper level prices accompanied with traditional department store services. McKenzies seeks to deliver excellent value and consistent, reliable service through stores located in suburban and urban markets, with a strong presence in the urban centres of Canadian cities. Bargos is Canada's leading mass merchandise discount chain of 327 outlets. Its mission is to provide Canada's "moms" and their families with fashion-right affordable products which are always in stock and always priced competitively. Specifically, each product is benchmarked against a national brand and priced 20 percent to 40 percent below it. Now, there is virtually no community of more than 3,000 people in Canada that is not within a five mile drive of a McKenzies or Bargos outlet.

To reduce costs, corporate services are shared between the two chains. This sharing includes logistics, distribution and transportation, information technology, credit, real estate, finance and accounting, legal services, human resources, global sourcing, and communications.

This week McKenzies entered the e-retailing business with a subsidiary "e-MB.com." The business model behind e-MB.com is that customers can order over the Internet from both chains and that delivery would be arranged through a third party parcel delivery company. Returns of products can be made at any outlet of either McKenzies or Bargos regardless of originating chain. This e-commerce venture is expected to lever the logistics, buying power, customer communications, and loyalty programs of the overall company. Moreover,

it allows the company to extend and deepen its customer relationship, offering the breadth of the company's combined merchandising strength to the total customer base. The catalogue business was discontinued decades ago, and thus there is no conflict with e-MB.com.

Required Prepare for the chair of the board of directors a plan based on margins and turnovers of how the three units (McKenzies, Bargos, and e-MB.com) will work in the foreseeable future. Expect there to be changes in product lines for each of the three units in order to maintain profitability.

Modern Chair

You have just started working for Modern Chair, a new organization that uses a modern, automated approach to the manufacture of a variety of chairs. Using computer-assisted design specifying and ordering materials and scheduling manual and machine activities, every chair can be unique, and Modern Chair can offer individual design on demand. Modern controls costs, which are lower than those of competitors who have less automation and less ability to efficiently produce small batches. Nevertheless, the success of the company has led to a problem. Currently with the economy in what looks to be a temporary boom, there is a shortage of capacity. There are no plans to expand production capacity to meet temporary excess demand. The president asked you for recommendations for making the best use of limited production capacity. Your recommendations are to facilitate profit maximization.

In your investigation, you realize that there is not much in the way of information on which to base the recommendations. The organization has little history, and the president has personally made all important decisions. You note, however, that besides the design department that has unlimited capacity, there are two production departments: the first department assembles the chairs, while the second does the finishing. Although there are 252 different types of chairs if all styles and finishes are considered, Modern divides them into two types, upholstered and straight back. Using this conceptualization, you allocate production costs according to assembly or finishing. Within each department, you further divide the costs according to upholstered or straight back chairs.

Then you take the cost for each product category in each department and run simple regressions, and get the results seen in Exhibit 1.

Each department's total available hours are 3,920 hours a year, i.e., 16 hours a day for 5 days a week for 49 weeks a year. The assembly department runs 5 identical lines. The yearly capacity is 19,600 operating hours. The finishing department runs 4 lines for 15,680 hours of available time. An average upholstered chair sells for $147 and the average straight back chair sells for $76. Sales of straight back chairs are unlikely to exceed 25,000 at that price, while that price will restrict upholstered chairs to 25,000. There is sufficient capacity in the assembly department, but not in the finishing department.

For each department, the standard hours in production needed to produce the chairs are:

	Upholstered	Straight Back
Assembly	0.75	0.50
Finishing	0.45	0.75

Modern occupied its current facilities four years ago. The assembly department cost $927,000 for plant and equipment. The finishing department's plant and equipment cost $554,000. About 80 percent was for equipment while the remaining 20 percent was for the land and buildings. Since then, the capacities of the two departments have increased about 5 or 6 percent a year. The managers and employees found ways to increase efficiency and effectiveness.

In examining the non-manufacturing costs, you find that they are all fixed except the 5 percent sales commission paid on the sales price of each chair.

Required You have just finished a nice lunch at Spartan's and are seeing the President of Modern Chair within an hour. Linear programming comes to your mind as being a suitable tool. What analysis and recommendation would you provide?

EXHIBIT 1

Variable	Coefficient	Standard Error
ASSEMBLY DEPARTMENT		
With the total costs of upholstered chairs as the dependent variable		
1. Constant	$ 98,747	$246,868
Independent variable: Time in production hours	$27.14	$11.81
$r^2 = 0.55$		
2. Constant	$352,363	$167,922
Independent variable: Direct labour hours	$11.74	$10.67
$r^2 = 0.33$		
With the total costs of straight back chairs as the dependent variable		
1. Constant	$347,428	$386,031
Independent variable: Time in production hours	$21.11	$ 6.60
$r^2 = 0.61$		
2. Constant	$797,318	$346,660
Independent variable: Direct labour hours	$ 5.06	$ 5.62
$r^2 = 0.35$		
FINISHING DEPARTMENT		
With the total costs of upholstered chairs as the dependent variable		
1. Constant	$ 27,957	$ 8,223
Independent variable: Time in production hours	$ 4.74	$ 1.16
$r^2 = 0.67$		
2. Constant	$ 54,819	$ 10,542
Independent variable: Direct labour hours	$ 3.51	$11.70
$r^2 = 0.31$		
With the total costs of straight back chairs as the dependent variable		
1. Constant	$155,850	$141,682
Independent variable: Time in production hours	$ 6.18	$ 1.29
$r^2 = 0.50$		
2. Constant	$347,310	$ 86,828
Independent variable: Direct labour hours	$ 3.57	$ 2.75
$r^2 = 0.33$		

PC-Board — Part 1

PC-Board Limited is a leading North American manufacturer of advanced printed circuit structures used in a variety of complex electronic applications. The company markets its products to major original equipment manufacturers (OEMs) and large contract assemblers in the telecommunications, computer, automotive, and industrial electronics industries. For example, the company currently manufacturers printed circuits for the latest generation of high-speed fibre optic switching stations, wireless communication sets, laptop computers, bar code reading systems, and electronic engine-control assemblies.

Investments

In recent years, there was significant investment in new manufacturing systems. In the past five years alone, the company invested more than $50 million in the most advanced manufacturing technology. Future investments are expected to be about $5 million per year for further automation of operations and the introduction of new processes.

Investment growth has been paralleled with enhancements to employee training and production quality. The company's commitment to human resource development includes continuous resource development, training, and re-skilling. The company's culture of quality, teamwork, and continuous learning was reinforced by an annual average of 80 hours of classroom and on-the-job training per employee.

The company's human resource and quality investments have been recognized. PC-Board's three plants satisfied the stringent requirements of the international standard for quality assurance management systems and obtained the ISO 9002 official registration from the Quality Management Institute. The company's major suppliers of primary materials and components also allowed their quality processes to be audited according to the ISO 9002 standards.

Prospects

Price increases are not expected from year to year, nor does the current business plan factor in any forecasted improvement in market conditions. The company is committed to internal improvements as a basis for sustained profit improvements. However, it will be possible to obtain higher average prices, through an improved product mix featuring a greater proportion of higher value-added products.

Accordingly, the most significant challenge is to further increase productivity as measured by the reduction of manufacturing cycle times. The manufacturing strategy is to optimize learning and therefore slide down the cost curves with the new technologies developed with customers.

The Cost Accounting System

PC-Board is dominated by engineers and marketers. The president, an electrical engineer, was advised by the external auditor to hire a controller that could develop management accounting systems that would be appropriate and cost effective. You are that controller, and you report to the president. Previously your position, up to a year ago when you joined the company, reported to the vice-president of marketing, and it was called the chief accountant.

Your present task is to review and make recommendations for the cost accounting system, which evolved with the last three chief accountants. Basically, the cost accounting system keeps track of the costs for producing an order. An order may take a few weeks or months to produce, and accounting reports are produced at regular intervals. Each order is made with selected operations undertaken by specialized capital equipment operated by skilled employees. Although, the orders differ, each product in a particular order will receive exactly identical amounts of the company's resources.

The cost accounting system compiles the costs by order. Direct materials and purchased components are charged to the order. Conversion cost (indirect costs and labour cost) are charged for each operation based on the time in production and other cost drivers. Actual conversion costs are charged to orders; however, the operations are well understood so that standard conversion costs could be used.

After examining the cost accounting system, the following recording practices are typical of what is employed for each order.

Materials, components inventories	XXX	
Accounts payable, cash		XXX
Work in process, operation 1	YYY	
Materials, components inventories control		YYY
Work in process, operation 1	ZZZ	
Conversion costs allocated		ZZZ
.		
.		
.		
Work in process, operation 9	VVV	
Conversion costs allocated		VVV
Finished goods	SSS	
Work in process		SSS
Cost of goods sold	PPP	
Finished goods		PPP

After your review, you discuss the accounting system with members of the accounting department. They believe the accounting system to be accurate, but they are concerned that the reports are not used regularly by the manufacturing and marketing departments. The newly promoted assistant controller expressed the frustration of the accounting department when she said, "We prepare timely and accurate reports on each operation in the sequence of producing an order, but not a single person cares."

The company is always trying to reduce costs, and thus with the cost accounting reports not being used, you wonder if they can be replaced with something less expensive. You then visit the manufacturing and marketing departments, and interview the 12 persons that receive the reports. The conclusion from these interviews is that these manufacturing and marketing decision makers only want the final cost of an order. At the end of the interview, the vice-president of manufacturing left you with the following assessment, "The accountants mean well with their detailed costs accounting by operation, but it is of no use to us. The money it costs for 90 percent of those reports is wasted."

Required As the controller, prepare a report to the vice-presidents of manufacturing and marketing addressing their assessment of the usefulness of the existing cost accounting system and make recommendations that will ensure they receive useful and cost-effective reports from the present, or an alternative, cost accounting system.

PC-Board — Part 2

The information in part 1 is relevant, and you are the controller. Now the president wants you to examine a recurring problem with the company's bidding process for new orders. As each order tends to be large, all senior managers are involved with the submission of bids. The accounting department constantly disagrees with the manufacturing department on bidding decisions. Typically, the company wants to earn a 30 percent profit margin on total costs, which both departments accept, however they disagree on some individual bids.

Position of Accounting Department

You examine the accounting department practices in costing bids. The department costs a possible order by including: materials, purchased components, and indirect costs. No direct labour is added as all labour is considered fixed. Thus, labour and other indirect costs are allocated with the most appropriate cost drivers. For example, set-up costs are allocated based on the number of set-ups, inspection by the number of inspections, assembly by the through put time, etc.

The accountants use an ABC system. Costs are assigned to activities based on use of resources, then assigned to cost objects, such as products, based on the use of activities. Six assumptions underlie the use of ABC. First, activities consume resources, and acquiring resources creates cost. Second, products or customers consume activities. A third assumption is that ABC models consumption rather than spending. This assumption's implication is perhaps the most important. For costs to decrease, there must be a change in spending. ABC, however, does not measure spending — it measures consumption. In the short run, a change in activity will have little or no impact on the consumption of resources. In the longer run, adjustments can be made to bring spending into alignment with consumption.

The fourth assumption, closely related to the first two, is that there are numerous causes for the consumption of resources. A further assumption, implicit in the fourth assumption, is that a wide array of activities can be identified and measured. These activities serve as linkages between the costs of resources and cost objects. The linkages enable multiple cost pools rather than a single cost pool to be used — reflecting a cause-and-effect relationship. A major advantage of ABC is the recognition that the activity measures can be organized into a hierarchy, namely:

- Unit-level activities which are performed each time a unit is produced,
- batch-level activities which are performed each time a batch of goods is produced,
- product-level activities which are performed as needed to support the production of each different type of product, and
- facility-level activities which simply sustain a facility's general manufacturing process.

A fifth assumption of ABC is that cost pools are homogeneous which means that for each cost pool there is only one activity. The implication is that there are many cost pools. The sixth and last assumption of ABC is that all costs in each pool are variable (strictly proportional to activity). When this assumption is coupled with the previous assumption of cost pool homogeneity, it becomes apparent that only costs considered "fixed" in the traditional sense would be "facility-level" activities.

Position of Manufacturing Department

The vice-president of manufacturing admits to the conflict that his department has with the accounting department. He is frustrated in not being able to reconcile what he believes with what the accounting department believes. This was less serious, he said, before the firm implemented ABC. In discussing the conflict with the vice-president of manufacturing, you realize that he views costs much differently than the accounting department. First, he is concerned with throughput contribution, which he defines as revenue minus the variable cost of materials, purchased components, and energy. He believes that all other costs are fixed, e.g., indirect manufacturing costs and all labour. Second, optimal performance to him is to maximize the throughput contribution. To maximize throughput, the vice-president is constantly eliminating or attempting to eliminate bottlenecks to allow production capacity to increase. For example, the vice-president removed a bottleneck with two machines in the group producing the fibre optic switching stations. These machines were bottlenecks, as they were operating a full capacity while other machines in the sequence were operating with unused capacity levels. The solution was to reduce the load of the bottleneck machines by shifting operations performed onto other machines. This increased total capacity for fibre optic switching stations by 12 percent.

The Bidding Process

Nearly all orders are obtained by winning bids, even with long-term clients. Orders vary in size from $2 to $40 million, with most in the $20 to $30 million range. The bidding committee consists of the president and the five vice-presidents, and yourself, the controller. In effect, the bidding committee is a formal means of working with the vice-president of marketing in her submission of bids. The committee ensures that all bids are appropriately priced and that if successful, the conditions of all bids are met.

In analyzing bids, the accountants cost the potential order by adding the actual costs of materials and purchased components to the cost of the required operations at the allocation rates established by ABC. A 30 percent markup is added to these costs to cover other overhead and profits. You the controller generally vote in favour of bids prepared by the vice-president of marketing when the price equals or exceeds the cost plus the 30 percent markup.

The manufacturing department analyzes all bids with throughput contribution. All bids and potential bids are ranked as to their total throughput contribution and according to the ratio of the throughput contribution to total variable cost of materials, purchased components, and energy.

Generally, there is agreement on about 80 percent of the bids. The accounting department generally rejects the remaining 20 percent because the markup is less than the 30 percent. Manufacturing generally votes in favour of these additional orders on the basis that those bids are competitive and that there is capacity to produce the orders. Moreover, the vice-president of manufacturing says that "If there are more orders, manufacturing is forced to find ways to increase capacity by eliminating bottlenecks. This increased capacity provides a larger base to allocate fixed costs." You believe the vice-president of manufacturing is genuine in what he believes, but now you are unsure how it reconciles with the ABC that your department uses with bids. However, you are going to have to reconcile the two systems for the president.

Investment Appraisal

The president has also asked you to evaluate a capital investment project put forth by the vice-president of manufacturing. The proposed $500,000 investment, in assets of the 30 percent CCA class, has a life of eight years after which the salvage value is $50,000. Annual operating costs will increase by $60,000 of which $10,000 is for amortization. However, the throughput contribution is expected to be $100,000 a year. The required rate of return is 10 percent and the income tax rate is 45 percent. The tax shield rate formula is shown below.

$$\text{Tax Shield Rate} = \frac{T \times C}{C + R} \; \frac{2 + R}{2(1 + R)}$$

where,

C = the CCA rate
R = the after tax required rate of return
T = the income tax rate

Required Complete the assignment for the president. Be sure to explain why there is a conflict between the manufacturing and accounting departments, and provide recommendations for resolving the conflict so that the bidding committee can make the best short-run and long-run decisions for PC-Board. Also, include in your report an analysis of the capital project and a recommendation to accept or reject it.

Precious Metals

Just after their December examinations, four management accounting students — who had been team members in a management accounting course — met to consider an equity investment. A relative — a young mining engineer — had asked one member to evaluate a mining proposal, offering him the opportunity to become a shareholder.

This new venture was to mine precious metal on a property that had in the past been considered to have too small of an ore body to be economically viable. Located about 500 kilometres north of Toronto, the mine in question is close to good roads. Moreover, as there is substantial unemployment in the area from the closure of other mines, appropriately skilled workers, with an expected average wage of $22 per hour, are plentiful. Five years ago, when unemployment levels in the province were low, an average wage of $25 might not attract the required labour force.

Recent changes in the technology of mining equipment have made economical the mining of smaller properties. Diamond drilling surveying was done for the property's ore body. The survey concluded that the property has sufficient ore for a mine and processing plant operating 20 years at 1,500,000 tonnes (1 tonne = 1,000 kilograms) per year. The expected yield is 0.05 percent, i.e., for every tonne there will be 0.5 kilograms of the precious metal.

The mining engineer estimated the equipment and plant at $38 million. Of the total assets, half has a CCA rate of 30 percent, one third has a CCA rate of 20 percent and the remaining one-sixth has a CCA rate of 10 percent. The assets will last for the life of the ore body, after which time the expected salvage value is $2 million; only assets subject to 30 percent CCA are salvageable.

The estimated processing costs (excluding amortization or capital cost allowance) are $16 a tonne. Estimated administrative and selling costs are $4 million and $1 million per year respectively. Working capital requirements are $1 million. An added initial investment of $1 million will recover other trace minerals. This would amount to 100,000 kilograms a year at 10 percent of the kilogram price of the precious metal. Operating costs and other costs would increase by 10 cents a tonne. There is no expected salvage value for these assets which are in the 30 percent CCA class.

The mining engineer has spent $100,000 for the property, diamond drilling, incorporation, and solicitation for investors. The company must reimburse her upon start up. She is also considering the idea of asking $5 million for the company.

The price per kilogram of the precious metal is likely to fluctuate because the metal is a material for luxury goods that varies in demand and price directly with the North American economy. A consulting economist used probability analysis to present estimates of future prices.

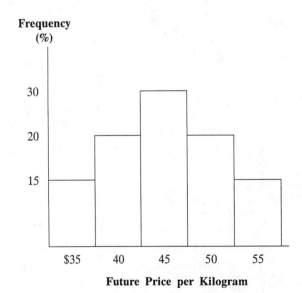

Future Price per Kilogram

Precious Metals is a typical mining company. Its key success factors are market price for the metal, yield of the ore, and operating costs per tonne of ore.

There is to be a board of directors to whom the general manager (i.e., the young mining engineer) would report. This reporting amounts to board approval of the 20-year plan. The board also approves the annual budget, and reviews the quarterly performance in comparison to the budget. Otherwise, the general manager has complete autonomy in managing the mine. The team members have two other concerns: (1) risk inherent in fluctuations, and (2) that the young mining engineer will run the mine for her benefit and not the owners. You and your team members had a long discussion about how the owners could be assured that she made decisions best for the company and not just herself. While the team members believed her to be honest, they all believed that differences in objectives could put the interests of the investors in jeopardy.

The discount rate (R) is 8 percent after tax. The income tax (T) rate is 40 percent. Calculate the tax shield with the following equation (C is the CCA rate). For the first year, the half-year rule applies, and it is shown as the second part of the equation.

$$\text{Tax Shield Rate} = \frac{T \times C}{C + R} \frac{2 + R}{2(1 + R)}$$

Required

1. Evaluate the investment opportunity with a discounted cash flow technique.
2. How would you control the costs in developing the property for production so that the objectives of the owners are being incorporated into decisions and actions?
3. How would you control the general manager after the start of production so that the objectives of the owners are being incorporated into decisions and actions?

Realwood Decks

Rene LaBlanc started Realwood Decks after he finished his degree in business administration. Although, he had not planned to go into business, the lack of suitable jobs forced the choice. The deck business was an obvious choice as during summers he worked for a deck contractor. Realwood supplies wood decks for homeowners. Rene chose the retail side in order not to directly compete with and offend his summer employer, his uncle.

The demand for wood decks has some distinctive patterns. First, the demand is very cyclical. Deck expenditures are very discretionary. During recessionary times the demand shrinks dramatically, while during times when employment is high and money readily available, the demand is very strong. Consequently, annual sales of Realwood can vary by 10 to 20 percent a year.

The second is the existence of a strong seasonal pattern. Decks are for summer, and the installation of decks is done with that in mind. Warmer months are more conducive to the necessary outside installation activities. As a result, there are marked differences in expected sales among the various months of the year as to expected sales. The following exhibit shows the seasonal factors. Expressed in percentage terms, the monthly factor shows the relation to an average month.

Seasonal Factors

April	177.8
May	204.2
June	199.7
July	131.3
August	122.6
September	69.4
October	55.1
November	51.3
December	39.0
January	42.9
February	47.5
March	59.2

The advantage of seasonal adjustment is that the sales of one month can be compared to earlier months and not just to the same month the year earlier. As a result, seasonally adjusted sales figures can reveal the sales trend six months earlier than unadjusted figures. This lead time in figuring out cyclical patterns is crucial for maintaining adequate, but not excessive inventories.

Realwood operates by ordering lumber and hardware from suppliers. These materials must be available for cutting to rough or exact lengths when demanded by customers. Of total customers, 60 percent are the ultimate consumers (the homeowner) and 40 percent are contractors. The sales breakdown is 5 percent hardware, 75 percent pressure treated wood, and 20 percent cedar. Gross margins are 50 percent, 40 percent, and 45 percent, respectively. It takes about two weeks from ordering to receiving supplies, and two months supply is necessary at the beginning of a month to ensure adequate selection. Selling and administration costs are fixed at $12 million per year, with nearly no monthly variation, with a variable part equal to 4 percent of sales.

As a shareholder and part-time accountant for Realwood, it is your responsibility to budget the sales and purchases of lumber and hardware for the next year. It is now March 12 and the budget is due April 1, the first day of the new fiscal year. With the economy in Realwood's trading area coming out of a recession, next year's sales are likely to be 15 percent more than the current year. The longer term growth rate is 5 percent per year for nominal sales.

You have identified your work as follows:

1. Prepare the sales budget for the next fiscal year, and using the seasonal factors, convert the annually budgeted sales into budgeted sales for each month.

2. With the benefit of seasonally adjusted monthly sales, examine the trend over the last five years to decide the validity of the projected 15 percent improvement.

EXHIBIT 1

REALWOOD DECKS
Monthly and Annual Sales
Year Ending March 31*

	1997	1998	1999	2001	2001
April	$ 5.94	$ 6.31	$ 6.65	$ 6.60	$ 5.86
May	6.90	7.25	7.66	7.52	6.82
June	6.83	7.11	7.57	7.31	6.61
July	4.46	4.74	4.96	4.73	4.41
August	4.24	4.46	4.71	4.36	4.08
September	2.40	2.55	2.69	2.44	2.37
October	1.91	2.02	2.14	1.91	1.87
November	1.82	1.90	2.02	1.76	1.76
December	1.37	1.44	1.56	1.35	1.37
January	1.53	1.61	1.71	1.48	1.53
February	1.71	1.76	1.84	1.57	1.71
March	2.11	2.33	2.29	1.99	2.20
Total of the Year	41.22	43.36	45.79	43.02	40.59
Inventory, Year End	12.81	13.10	13.66	14.05	14.25

* The sales for March 31, 2001 are estimated.

3. Comment on the timing of turning points using seasonally adjusted sales compared to those using only monthly sales for the current month compared to the year earlier.

4. Specify the amounts and timing of orders from suppliers to ensure the sales demand is met.

In preparing the budget, a major concern is with the level of sales by month for the total year. Exhibit 1 displays the monthly and annual sales for the last five years.

Required Complete your work.

Royal Trust

Required You just joined a major stock brokerage firm. As a condition of your employment contract, you were hired as a research analyst with duties to analyze companies and make recommendations as to whether the shares of certain companies should be bought, held, or sold. Your contract also specified that after one year of experience with the firm, you would become the analyst responsible for banks and financial institutions. On the first day, the director of research asked you to use past annual reports and stock price patterns to explain, with the case analysis approach, the 1993 demise of Royal Trust. He explained that Royal Trust had been a very successful firm over most of its long life, but in a relatively short period of time it had run into problems that were not satisfactorily resolved.

You start by gathering together the Royal Trust annual reports for the 1983 to 1992 period along with monthly stock prices. The following sections are summaries of what you learned about Royal Trust.

Annual Report Narratives

The Royal Trust Company ceased operations in 1993. The Royal Bank, an unrelated company, purchased its trust operations and the name Royal Trust; the remaining assets were placed in a new firm called Gentra Inc. This was the end of a 94-year life for Royal Trust; it was also the end of a 10-year period where Trilon Financial Corporation, a financial holding company, was the major shareholder.

In 1983, Trilon Financial Corporation came to own directly and indirectly just over 50 percent of the shares of Royal Trust. Upon acquiring majority ownership of Royal Trust, Trilon installed a new chairman, Mr. J. Trevor Eyton, and a new president and chief executive officer, Mr. Michael Cornelissen.

Chairman Eyton announced two new committees in his 1983 annual report message to shareholders in addition to the "usual complement of board of directors' committees." The first was the business conduct review committee, which was charged with preparing and monitoring an updated code of business conduct, reviewing business ethics within the company, and resolving any conflict of interest situations applicable to employees, directors, and major shareholders. The directors on this committee were to be independent of the major shareholders, Trilon. The second committee was the investment review committee which was to consist of seven directors, with the majority being "unaffiliated shareholders directors." The duties of this committee included the review of investment decisions and policies for both client and corporate funds, and any investment decisions involving a major shareholder, affiliated company, or a company with which any director, officer or employee is affiliated.

Although appointed president and chief executive officer only in August 1983, by October of that year Mr. Cornelissen had, according to his message in the annual report, completed a clearly defined and detailed business plan that had been approved by the board of directors. In addition he announced that:

> Policies and objectives for all business segments were defined. Lines of communication have been shortened and simplified to ensure a closeness of senior management to products and services, and to the needs of clients. We have increased our expectations of the standards of performance of our employees and advisors.

If the above were not enough, Cornelissen also announced in his annual report message that there would be a management share purchase plan to commit senior management to shareholder interests, namely:

The board of directors has approved a share purchase plan and a share option plan subject to approval by the shareholders at the annual meeting. The plans are designed to ensure senior management commitment to the long term strategic goals and objectives of the company in a manner consistent with shareholder interests.

The annual report for 1984 had Hartland Molson MacDougall give the chairman's report. The previous chairman, Eyton, resigned in October 1984. MacDougall mentioned that Royal Trust had advantages because its parent, Trilon, also owned London Life, Wellington Insurance, and Royal LePage. He did not elaborate or explain these advantages.

Cornelissen's 1984 president's message announced that five important initiatives were undertaken during the past year: (1) a commitment to quality, (2) the arrest and reverse of the past erosion in market share suffered in certain major product lines, (3) a major catch-up with necessary expenditures in computer systems development and marketing, (4) the conservative recapitalization of the company, and (5) the development of a new business planning process. The latter accomplishment was done by restructuring — i.e., a separation of the company's operations into personal financial services and corporate financial services — in order to be closer to the customer. Cornelissen announced that this would reduce up to five layers of management throughout the company. He also announced six new senior executives, and that an "innovative" employee compensation plan had been designed for implementation in 1985 to "ensure that deserving employees are well rewarded for superior performance against high expectations and standards we set for ourselves." No other details were given.

MacDougall noted in the 1985 annual report that there was a "new Royal Trust" that was bolder and stronger

> ...with a board of directors who represent the highest standards of business practice and ethics, and a senior management who have established not only clear objectives but also the strategies for achieving our priorities. I am fully confident that the new Royal Trust, with its direct focus on people — our managers, employees, shareholders, and especially, our clients — is well prepared to achieve our goal of being Canada's premier provider of financial services.

Cornelissen's message for the 1985 annual report reiterated his earlier commitment to quality, market focus, and computer systems. He also noted the goal to improve linkages with other members of the Trilon group of companies. He elaborated on the pay for performance programs, which he called "unique." Specifically, he noted there were three incentive plans — the management incentive option, the employee bonus plan, and the employee share thrift plan — and that they were an integral part of the company's performance management process. Otherwise, few specific details were given about these programs.

MacDougall announced in his 1986 annual report message that the company established a representative office in Tokyo, and, most significantly, acquired Dow Financial Services Corporation. Dow added to the company's asset management and merchant and private banking services in Switzerland, U.K., Hong Kong and Singapore. Cornelissen announced that the acquisition of Dow more than doubled the company's international operations. He also announced the four major objectives of the current five-year plan: (1) to substantially increase deposits, (2) to double mortgage lending activities, (3) to increase fee income from personal and corporate financial services to 50 percent of net income, and (4) to achieve 15 percent growth in earnings per common share while maintaining conservative capital ratios consistent with high credit ratings. These objectives were to be achieved by investing in technology to create cost-efficient deposit, lending and trust systems; obtaining new and improved branch locations, domestically and overseas; and further exploiting opportunities within the Trilon group of companies. Towards the end of his message, Cornelissen noted succinctly that the expansion would need to come from new sources, i.e., "(t)he planned 15 percent earnings growth and 15 to 20 percent return on equity means business growth will have to come, in part, from new and different sources in the years to come."

The most significant part of MacDougall's 1987 chairman's letter was not the content but the quote from a brokerage firm inserted in the margin:

> ...shareholders' interests are shared by senior management whose compensation combines significant share ownership with modest fixed salaries. This arrangement reaffirms management's commitment to long term earnings growth.

The comment came from an analyst from Walwyn, Stodgell Cochran Murray who apparently favourably viewed the Royal Trust management incentive program for managers. It appears the chairman, MacDougall, thought this approval was important to communicate to shareholders. In other words, the chairman appeared to want to communicate the stock market's approval of Royal Trust's incentive program for managers.

Cornelissen's message stressed the successes of Royal Trust. The quotes in the margin of his president's message communicated what he apparently thought was important. The Canadian Bond Rating Service was quoted as saying:

[Royal Trust's] primary strength has been their ability to maintain consistent growth in earnings over the past five years while maintaining a quality oriented balance sheet. Throughout this time period profitability ratios have been superior to the industry average despite their conservative leverage ratios and accounting policies.

Andreas Research Capital Inc. was quoted as saying:

[Royal Trust] management has a sense of purpose and vision of the future and a credible plan to maximize the company's potential that are unparalleled in the financial services industry in Canada. Moreover, the company's senior management has greater rewards for superior achievement and greater penalties for failure than that of any other financial services company.

On the page following Cornelissen's report, there was a Walwyn, Stodell Cochran Murray quote:

In 1983, [Royal Trust] brought a new 'entrepreneurial driven' senior management who have concentrated on creating a more productive culture. The company's organizational structure was simplified making it less bureaucratic than it was before and much less than its main competitors, the banks.

MacDougall and Cornelissen announced another good year in the 1988 annual report. The latter explained these good results with the following:

Royal Trust's sixth consecutive year of record performance again results from the hard work, enthusiasm and energy of our employees. We foster a corporate culture which lets our people's talents and

initiatives flourish. The glue that binds us is our shared values. ... We shun hierarchies and bureaucracy. We encourage and reward team players who are willing to take soundly based risks with personal accountability for results. We operate through informal networks and work groups defined by clients' needs rather than internal organization considerations.

This explanation for the successful year was similar to that given by Cornelissen in the prior year. Expansion activities were also described by Cornelissen. This included the introduction of private banking services in Montreal, Toronto, and Vancouver; and new banking, investment and trust operations in Austria, Luxembourg, British Virgin Islands, Isle of Man and Barbados. Furthermore, after the year end (February 6, 1989) Royal Trust acquired Pacific First Financial Corporation of Tacoma, Washington in the United States. Cornelissen also reported on the company's performance against objectives. Apparently all objectives had been achieved in the past year.

For the second year, Cornelissen's report included quotes from market watchers. For example, Wood Gundy Inc. was quoted saying:

[Royal Trust] is an outstanding, full-service financial services company which should continue to prosper in the de-regulated marketplace. Given the company's strategy and its management's strong personal and financial commitment to company goals, [Royal Trust]'s business fundamentals are excellent.

The Financial Post was quoted as saying:

Like a well-oiled machine, [Royal Trust] of Toronto continues to produce steady growth in revenue and earnings with enviable consistency.

Instead of a message from the chairman in the 1989 annual report, there was tribute to him entitled, "Royal Trust's Secret Weapon." The subtitle read, "Far from using his chairmanship to slow his pace, Hartland MacDougall now works harder than ever." The tribute ended with,

That he is modest about these accomplishments is indicative of a basic humility evident in his every action. He believes honesty and integrity are the most important values in his business. This may explain, in part, his forthrightness. Untiring, enthusiastic and personable, Hartland MacDougall is indeed Royal Trust's "secret weapon."

Cornelissen's message to the shareholders summarized the great successes that had occurred for Royal Trust since 1983.

The 1990 annual report had some differences. MacDougall and Cornelissen, were now calling themselves, respectively, managing partner, chairman and managing partner, chief executive officer. MacDougall and Cornelissen started the annual report with a "partner tribute" where they admitted that "1990 was the toughest year we have faced since we joined Royal Trust" and that they we proud of "the tireless dedication and loyalty of our employee partners." They then discussed how the "partnership" led "Royal Trusters" to more effectively work together to meet client needs:

Partnership evolved naturally from our non-bureaucratic, flat organizational structure that allows us to be immediately responsive to client needs. It empowers every partner to break down any barrier that blocks his or her ability to provide superior service. In 1990, partnership changed the way we think about each other and the way we work together.

The 1990 annual report also signalled the use of new terms for describing organizational positions; the traditional job titles of vice-president, director and manager were replaced with managing partner, partner and associate partner. In a section beside the partner tribute, these new titles were described as connoting an individual's level of accountability.

In his chairman's message, MacDougall put the bulk of the blame for poor performance on the "rapidly deteriorating economic conditions in Canada and the United Kingdom." This justification was evident in explaining the problem with the U.K. business, namely,

Our policy was to be conservative and risk averse. However, some of the loans we made then could not withstand the rigours of a downturn. Skyrocketing interest rates, inflation and a severely depressed real estate market resulted in problem loans for the entire U.K. banking system and we unfortunately were no exception.

In his message, Cornelissen noted that Royal Trust was "solid to the core" and that the loss of

$65 million or $1.20 per share was the result of several factors: (1) a cyclical economy leading to an increase in mortgage defaults; (2) a combination of prolonged high rates, a steeply depressed property market in the U.K. bringing with it massive loan losses throughout the entire U.K. banking industry; (3) a severe decline in the Japanese stock market which caused investment losses in Switzerland; (4) deterioration in the value of a portfolio of U.S. equities created in 1987 to build relationships with the management of those companies.

In the 1991 annual report, MacDougall noted that 1992 would be a year of opportunity, and that it was 100 years since Royal Trust was granted a charter and 92 years since it opened its first branch. However, he said little about the past year's performance of the company.

Cornelissen said in his message to the shareholders that 1991 was one of the most difficult years for many industries as they experienced the rigours of the worst economic recession since World War II. The year, he said, was devoted to focussing on improving credit controls, reducing expenses, and building on existing strengths. More significant steps included: restructuring European operations, and the discontinuity of certain new construction loans in California. He also included Royal Trust's statement on culture and values which emphasized entrepreneurial behaviour and adherence to the goals of the owners.

In the annual report for 1992, there was a joint message to shareholders by MacDougall and James Miller, the new president and chief executive officer (the managing partner titles were, apparently, no longer used by the chairman and president). They tersely reported a net loss of $852 million compared with net income of $107 million for the previous year. On a common share basis, the loss was $5.93. They blamed the losses on economic conditions. They also noted:

... the Corporation retained S.G. Warburg to carry out an extensive review of the Corporation's operations and condition and to assist the Corporation, with the cooperation of Trilon Financial Corporation, the Corporation's largest shareholder, in assessing financial alternatives for the Corporation. It was hoped that a major financial institution would be willing to inject substantial new capital into the Corporation and a large number of financial institutions were approached on this basis.

Although a direct investment could not be arranged, the Corporation successfully entered into an Agreement in

Principle with Royal Bank of Canada in mid-March, under which Royal Bank has agreed in principle to purchase most of the Corporation's Canadian and international operations. A committee of independent directors has been formed to make a recommendation to the board with respect to the fairness of the proposed transaction to security holders.

The Agreement in Principle with Royal Bank has stabilized Royal Trust's business and has allowed the Corporation to direct its efforts toward regaining some of the business lost during 1992 and early 1993. We firmly believe that the Royal Bank deal was the best deal available to the Corporation and is far better than the alternatives.

With no indication of responsibility or regret, that was the last annual report of Royal Trust.

Was There a Recession?

After reviewing the annual reports, you want to assure yourself that there was a recession in 1990–1992 as stated by MacDougall and Cornelissen in their annual report messages. They had blamed the demise of Royal Trust on the recession. You examine a book from your economics course, *Self-Organizing Economy* by Paul Krugman, which says all of the major industrial countries shared the recessions of 1974–1975, 1979–1982, and 1990–1992. Statistics Canada shows the quarterly growth in gross domestic product on constant dollars for each of those recessions in the table shown on Exhibit 1.

You know that recessions are defined by quarters of negative growth. With only one quarter of negative growth, there was not really a recession during the 1974–1975 period. There were six quarters of negative growth with the 1979 to 1982 recession, and only four quarters of negative growth in the 1990–1992 recession. The data negates the statement by MacDougall and Cornelissen about the seriousness of the 1990–1992 recession.

Quantitative Analysis

You analyzed the Royal Trust balance sheets and income statements in Exhibit 2, and compiled the Excel spreadsheet in Exhibit 3. You noted that

EXHIBIT 1: QUARTERLY GROWTH OF GDP

Recession	Year	1st	2nd	3rd	4th
1974–1975	1974	1.0	0.3	0.9	0.6
	1975	−0.4	1.1	1.4	0.7
1979–1982	1979	1.1	1.3	0.5	1.2
	1980	0.4	−0.4	−0.9	1.2
	1981	2.5	0.9	−0.7	−0.5
	1982	−0.8	−1.4	−0.9	−0.9
1990–1991	1990	0.7	−0.3	−0.6	−0.9
	1991	−1.3	0.2	0.4	0.3
	1992	0.0	0.2	0.3	0.4

there were two main businesses. There was the fiduciary business when Royal Trust was looking after the assets of others. This business showed up as fee and other income on the income statement. As the assets belonged to clients, they were not shown on Royal Trust's balance sheet. The other was the lending business which meant money was raised through deposits and other forms of debt and equity, and then loaned or invested in securities, mortgages, loans and other investments. The revenue from this latter business was described as investment income. However, interest expenses and the provision of loan losses were subtracted from investment income to yield net investment income.

With your analysis you calculated the margin on investments, gross yield on average funds in use, and undertook other analyses. You also examined the 1983 to 1992 movement of Royal Trust common share prices, on the premise that the efficient market hypothesis predicted that share prices reflected all information about a firm. In other words, the share prices would have reflected important information about the health of a firm that were not contained in the annual reports or otherwise disclosed by the directors.

Exhibit 4 contains the share prices from 1983 to 1992. You discovered that the common prices of Royal Trust declined to virtually zero in 1993.

Preliminary Assessment

Your reading of the annual reports, financial statements, and stock price changes leads you to several opinions contrary to the narrative comments espoused in annual reports by the chairman and presidents.

EXHIBIT 2: FINANCIAL STATEMENTS

Consolidated Balance Sheet

($000,000s)

	1992	1991	1990	1989	1988	1987	1986	1985	1984	1983	1982
ASSETS											
Cash and short term investments	3,131	3,715	4,958	5,567	5,310	4,279	3,453	2,146	2,070	2,107	2,235
Securities	2,905	5,364	5,470	5,875	3,920	3,616	2,530	1,862	1,621	1,016	1,684
Mortgages, loans, investments	17,790	27,320	29,394	27,475	18,838	16,244	13,068	9,217	7,278	6,344	5,594
Other assets	417	1,127	1,124	909	444	379	295	228	188	167	280
Net assets of discontinued U.S. operations	871										
Total Assets	25,114	37,526	40,946	39,826	28,512	24,518	19,346	13,453	11,157	9,634	9,793
LIABILITIES AND SHAREHOLDERS' EQUITY											
Deposits and debt	22,484	33,798	37,127	36,358	25,906	22,372	17,566	12,010	10,128	9,048	9,248
Other Liabilities, deferred taxes	234	278	280	243	235	271	224	295	226	149	129
Total Liabilities	22,718	34,076	37,407	36,601	26,141	22,643	17,790	12,305	10,354	9,197	9,377
Minority interest	9	8	7	26	42	53	58	17	21	5	6
Subordinated notes and capital debentures	1,419	1,486	1,490	921	661	196	207	—	—	—	—
Shareholders' equity	968	1,956	2,042	2,278	1,668	1,626	1,291	1,131	777	432	410
Total Liabilities and Shareholders' Equity	25,114	37,526	40,946	39,826	28,512	24,518	19,346	13,453	11,152	9,634	9,793

EXHIBIT 2...cont'd

Consolidated Statement of Income
($000,000s)

	1992	1991	1990	1989	1988	1987	1986	1985	1984	1983	1982
INCOME											
Investment Income	2,476	3,348	4,916	3,685	2,763	2,218	1,828	1,470	1,204	1,065	1,255
Interest expense	2,124	2,864	3,995	2,907	2,103	1,638	1,351	1,108	987	866	1,061
Net investment income before provisions	352	484	921	778	660	580	477	362	217	199	194
Provision for loan losses	421	155	220	23	18	26	18	12	16	18	13
Net investment income (loss) after provisions for losses	(69)	329	701	755	642	554	459	350	201	181	181
Fees and other income	351	337	349	298	248	200	154	116	263	252	211
Total Income	282	666	1,050	1,053	890	754	613	466	464	433	392
OPERATING EXPENSES											
Salaries and benefits	296	281	369	268	232	187	162	131			126
Premises, computer and equipment	160	154	—	—	—	—	—	—			34
Commissions to real estate brokers/agents	—	—	30	—	—	—	—	—			84
Restructuring costs	—	—	84	—	—	—	—	—			—
Portfolio investments	179	167	461	334	275	233	168	129			101
Other	—	—	—	—	—	—	—	—			—
Total operating expenses	635	602	944	602	507	420	330	260	366	354	345
Other additions	—	—	—	—	—	—	—	—	—	—	3
INCOME (LOSS) BEFORE THE FOLLOWING	(353)	64	106	451	383	334	283	206	98	79	50
Write-off of goodwill	(93)	—	—	—	—	—	—	—	—	—	—
Sale of stock transfer/debt trusteeship businesses	—	21	—	—	—	—	—	—	—	—	—
Income (loss) before taxes, discontinued U.S. operations	(446)	85	106	451	383	334	283	206	98	79	50
Income taxes	213	19	171	186	171	146	129	93	14	18	5
Net income (loss) before discontinued operations	(659)	66	(65)	265	212	188	154	113	84	61	45
Net income (loss) from discontinued operations	(193)	41	—	—	—	—	—	—	—	—	(1)
Non-recurring Items	—	—	—	—	—	—	—	—	1	4	—
Dividends on non-convertible preferred shares	—	—	—	—	—	—	—	35	19	10	—
Dividends on Series A and B convertible preferred shares	—	—	—	—	—	—	—	—	2	3	—
Net income (loss) applicable to preferred shareholders	(55)	71	(86)	74	56	58	51	35	21	13	10
Net income (loss) applicable to common shareholders	(907)	36	(151)	191	156	130	103	78	64	52	34
Net income (loss) after income taxes	(852)	107	(65)	265	212	188	154	113	85	65	44
Average number of shares outstanding (000,000's)	153	145	125	112	105	102	94	83	77	70	70
Earnings (loss) per common share — basic ($)	(5.93)	0.25	(1.21)	1.71	1.48	1.28	1.10	0.94	0.83	0.74	0.49

EXHIBIT 3: VARIOUS ANALYSES

	1992	1991	1990	1989	1988	1987	1986	1985	1984	1983
Margin (net investment income/investment income)	(0.028)	0.098	0.143	0.205	0.232	0.250	0.251	0.239	0.167	0.170
Gross yield on average funds in use	0.093	0.099	0.144	0.131	0.130	0.125	0.137	0.147	0.148	0.146
Interest cost (including losses)	0.095	0.089	0.124	0.104	0.100	0.094	0.103	0.112	0.123	0.121
Net yield on average funds in use	(0.003)	0.010	0.021	0.027	0.030	0.031	0.034	0.035	0.025	0.025
ROG, securities, mortgages, loans, investments	(0.369)	(0.063)	0.045	0.465	0.146	0.273	0.408	0.245	0.209	0.011

EXHIBIT 4: MONTHLY STOCK PRICE ACTIVITIES ($)

	1992	1991	1990	1989	1988	1987	1986	1985	1984	1983	1982
High price	9.38	11.25	16.13	19.38	17.63	18.50	17.32	11.88	9.20	7.38	5.10
Low price	2.40	7.77	8.13	15.88	12.75	11.00	10.75	8.88	5.94	4.75	2.88
Close for Year	2.94	8.00	9.00	17.88	16.38	13.88	14.82	11.75	9.00	7.38	4.97

Note: Share pries were adjusted in splits

SBS Books

SBS is one of North America's largest book retailers. In the early 1970s it was formed by the amalgamation of two established booksellers that had 90 stores in regional malls. Subsequently SBS expanded into a wider variety of retail outlets. There are now 27 superstores, 800 mall stores, and 285 campus bookstores.

The mall stores are 4,000 to 5,000 square feet each and profitable, but have little chance of above average growth. The campus stores are less profitable, but with average profitability they provide advertisement for SBS's other stores. It is the superstores that Dino Giovanni, the president and chief executive officer, expects to provide SBS's growth during the next decade. He is so confident that he changed the firm's name to SBS (for Superbook Stores). And in the last two years, he has experimented with a number of concepts to make the superstores exciting places to be and thereby attractive to customers.

Dino's superstore idea calls for 40,000 square foot destination book stores. Books are sold at discounts of 10 to 40 percent, and each store may have a many as 100,000 titles. Variations to the base store that have been tested include a juvenile book section, a children's book section, a children's activity centre with supervised baby sitting, a restaurant, and an espresso bar. Although stores will vary because the exact location and premises, the following describes the envisaged superstore:

	sq. ft.
Base store	27,000
Juvenile section increment	4,000
Children section increment	3,000
Children's activity centre	1,500
Restaurant	3,000
Espresso bar	1,500
	40,000

Real estate is purchased and/or developed to superstore specifications, and then sold to various pension funds. These properties are, in turn, rented. The belief is that SBS can earn above average return as a book retailer, but property ownership can only yield average returns. Moreover, SBS does not want to tie up its limited financial resources in real estate.

This lack of land and buildings means that there are minimal fixed assets on the balance sheet. The only significant item is leasehold improvement, which individual store managers have no control over. Moreover, cash management, regarding cash balances, accounts receivable, accounts payable, and bank loans, is done entirely by the treasurer. As there is a lack of influence over most balance sheet items, the return on investment (ROI) measure for performance at the store level has come to be calculated as operational income (before interest expenses, corporate allocations, and income taxes) divided by average annual book inventory. Currently, Dino is requiring all aspects of the superstores to earn at least a 20 percent ROI. This demanding target necessitates a skilful blend of profit margin on sales and inventory turnover. There is concern that ROI may not always be appropriate for measuring performance.

As a corporate management accountant, you have been assigned to analyse the profitability of the base store and the variations, and make recommendations to Dino on the size and composition of the superstores and the exclusive use of ROI. You have gathered the following information, which is believed to be representative of future potentials.

Base Store

Sales	$9,450,000
Cost of goods sold	5,670,000
Gross margin	3,780,000
Wages, administration, rent, utilities	3,240,000
Operational income	$ 540,000
Sales to average book inventory	7

Juvenile Section

Revenue	$1,100,000
Cost of goods sold	605,000
Gross margin	495,000
Wages, administration, rent, utilities	445,000
Operational income	$ 50,000
Sales to average book inventory	5

Children's Section

Sales	$720,000
Cost of goods sold	432,000
Gross margin	288,000
Wages, administration, rent, utilities	280,000
Operational income	$ 8,000
Sales to average book inventory	4

Children's Activity Centre

Revenue	$ 125,000
Wages, administration, rent, utilities	240,000
Operational income	$(115,000)

The average charge is $5 per child. On average the parent(s) of each child was found by a survey to have bought $10 worth of books strictly because of the babysitting offered by the children's activity centre. The variable costs of these books are 70 percent of the sales value.

Restaurant

Sales	$525,000
Food, supplies	210,000
Wages, administration, rent, utilities	400,000
Operational income	$(85,000)

The average bill was $9 per customer. On average each of these customers was found by a survey to have bought $10 worth of books strictly because of the restaurant. The variable costs of these books are 70 percent of the sales value.

Espresso Bar

Sales	$300,000
Food, supplies	90,000
Wages, administration, rent, utilities	260,000
Operational income	$(50,000)

The average bill was $6 per customer. On average each of these customers was found by a survey to have bought $15 worth of books strictly because of the espresso bar. The variable costs of these books are 70 percent of the sales value.

Required As the corporate management accountant, perform the duties assigned by the president. Use the case approach for this assignment.

Southern Computer Machines

Four decades ago, Southern Computer Machines (SCM) started as a manufacturer of semiconductors. However, two decades ago, SCM moved into PC manufacturing as a means of reducing the impact of cyclical semiconductor sales. Now with two successful businesses, analysts at major brokerage firms say the stock market perceives SCM to be only a PC fabricator. The market's perception leads the board of directors to question whether the present divisional structure is the most appropriate for ensuring optimal returns to shareholders' investments. They are sufficiently concerned that they have hired you as a consultant to address the questions of whether the semiconductor division should be (1) kept as currently operated, (2) sold outright, (3) sold through an initial public offering (IPO) to the public, or (4) spun off by distributing the shares to existing shareholders.

Semiconductor Industry

You soon learn from a review of the literature and brokerage reports that since its inception, the semiconductor industry has never been able to defy business cycles that swing wildly between boom and bust. Although chip sales have increased at a steady 17 percent rate annually compounded, manufacturing capacity has grown in fits and starts, always lagging behind or exceeding demand. The present boom, which dates back two years, is no exception. For this year, analysts are projecting a 77 percent semiconductor industry-wide profit surge. Until a few weeks ago, most analysts on Bay Street and Wall Street assumed that good times would last two more years, or until chip capacity outpace demand. Prices would then decline substantially. Nevertheless, short-term indicators were positive. Most chips were in severe shortage and prices were holding firm or trending up. Simultaneously the Philadelphia Semiconductor Stock Index jumped 68 percent in the six months that ended two weeks ago.

Then early last week two Wall Street chip analysts cautioned that the industry could peak within six months. Among the warning signs noted by the analysts were: creeping inventory levels, scattered price declines, and shorter waits to obtain some parts. Other Wall Street and Bay Street analysts fired back with counter-arguments, but to little avail; semiconductor stocks fell 20 percent on the Philadelphia Semiconductor Stock Index in the past week. One Bay Street analyst summed up the situation, "This is a cyclical industry, and nobody wants to be the last one out."

With further investigation you see evidence that the investors may have bailed out too early. The industry has changed to where it is no longer as monolithic as it was five years ago, when the semiconductors used in PCs set the pace. The demand has become much more diversified. Now it derives most of its growth from new markets such as Internet equipment and consumer electronics — everything from data switches and cell phones to digital cameras and DVD players. Consequently, the past extreme cycles are unlikely to be repeated.

The semiconductor industry association has provided some forecasts that indicate attractive future sales. The association says that five years ago, microprocessor and dynamic memory chips, largely used in PCs, provided 39 percent of all semiconductor revenues. In five years from now, the association expects semiconductors for PCs to represent only 25 percent of total sales. The non-PC semiconductors will be the fastest-growing sector, especially those used in communications products and optical parts used with the Internet backbone.

Semiconductor Division

Although the semiconductor division can assume responsibility for a product at any stage of development, OEMs (original equipment manufacturers) benefit most when partnering with the division at the early phases of design. Early involvement with the division's technology solutions, manufacturing and operations, and global services business unit helps to ensure a smooth, rapid and cost-effective transition from product concept to volume manufacturing. Before the division begins manufacturing any product, technology "roadmaps" are established to ensure the best decisions are made. In other words, this process ensures the assembly of functional, quality products that are efficiently manufactured, tested, and serviced.

Depending on the semiconductor product being manufactured, the division's technology solutions business unit is poised to provide a wide range of services including design of custom-integrated circuits and design coordination with the respective OEM. In addition, the division has broad-level design and physical layout capabilities for chip and circuit board assembly. Due to past alliances with router, cell phone, and PC manufacturers, the division now provides a complete array of chips and related products for these market areas.

The fact that the semiconductor division and the PC division are related has created some problems for the semiconductor division. Many potential PC fabricators are reluctant to buy semiconductors from the semiconductor division when they must compete for sales with its sister PC division. Other PC fabricator customers threaten to drop the division because of its association with the PC division. In addition, many of the PC division's major customers perceive there to be an ethical quandary whenever the PC division uses chips from the semiconductor division.

The business model is unclear for the semiconductor division. The division is very good at dealing with suppliers and customers. However, it is merely mediocre with the assembly of semiconductors. This confusion is reflected in its financial performance depicted in Exhibit 1.

PC Division

The PC division was started as a means of selling semiconductors. With this purpose, there was a reluctance to becoming a full-fledged manufacturing and sales firm. As a result the PC division outsourced almost everything from sales to

---

EXHIBIT 1: FINANCIAL SUMMARY — SEMICONDUCTOR DIVISION

Balance Sheet

Current Assets			Current Liabilities		
Cash, equivalent	$ 543		Accounts payable		$ 2,146
Net receivables	1,678		Accruals		452
Inventories	2,195		Other current liabilities		848
Other current assets	326				3,446
	4,742				
Long-term Assets			Long-term Liabilities and Owners' Equity		
Other investments	878		Long-term debt		5,249
Net property, plant and equipment	4,732		Deferred income		123
Intangible assets	87		Deferred taxes		223
	5,697		Other liabilities		56
			Owners' equity		1,744
					6,993
Total	$10,439		Total		$10,439

Income Statement

Net sales		$11,757
Less: Cost of goods sold		7,054
Gross income		4,703
Less: Amortization	769	
Selling and administration	3,000	
Total		3,769
Operating income		934
Other income or expenses		(200)
Pre-tax income		734
Income taxes		235
Net income		$ 499

manufacturing (except for the semiconductors that can be made by the semiconductor division), to research and development. The PC division's business model had invested significantly in supplier assets, which it then linked to its customer assets using the Internet and its organizational know-how and systems. Consequently, the PC division enables customers to access sales and service on its Web site. Its network of linked suppliers makes it possible for the company to efficiently tailor PC products to fit the needs of individual buyers, whether for a home-based PC for the employees, or with a global company.

Thus, the division was quick to become Web-based for sales and customer service operation. It has no traditional distribution network standing between itself and its customers. Customers are served by a telephone or an on-line order taker who actually works for a division of a telephone company. The order is sent to a coordinator — actually an employee who works for another company, Supplyex — who in turn passes the order to the relevant plant from among the division's five assembly plants around the world. At the same time, Supplyex directs parts suppliers of the required parts to the selected assembly plant. Supplyex also directs the parcel courier to the respective plant at the predetermined time to pick up and then deliver the finished computer to the customer.

The division depends on its ability to optimize all assets that make up its business model, including relationships with employees, suppliers, investors, and customers. This clarity of business model is reflected in the PC division's financial performance depicted in Exhibit 2.

Options for the Semiconductor Division

After reviewing the semiconductor division, you suggest that the division has to clarify its business model to improve performance. It does not focus on what it does best.

EXHIBIT 2: FINANCIAL SUMMARY — PERSONAL COMPUTER DIVISION

Balance Sheet

Current Assets		Current Liabilities	
Cash, equivalent	$2,066	Accounts payable	$1,769
Net receivables	1,339	Accruals	168
Inventories	196	Other current liabilities	659
Other current assets	240		2,596
	3,841		
Long-term Assets		Long-term Liabilities and Owners' Equity	
Other investments	1,446	Long-term debt	254
Net property, plant and equipment	382	Deferred income	135
Intangible assets	66	Deferred taxes	—
	1,894	Other liabilities	96
		Owners' equity	2,654
			3,139
Total	$5,735	Total	$5,735

Income Statement

Net sales		$12,632
Less: Cost of goods sold		9,941
Gross income		2,691
Less: Amortization	78	
Selling and administration	1,180	
Total		1,258
Operating income		1,433
Other income or expenses, net		(3)
Pre-tax income		1,430
Income taxes		393
Net income		$ 1,037

Required As the consultant, specify how the semiconductor division can clarify its business model and improve profits. Also, specify the advantages and disadvantages from each of the options, i.e., (1) keep as a division, (2) sell outright, (3) sell through an initial public offering (IPO) to the public, or (4) spin off by distributing the shares to existing shareholders.

Yoour University

Your first job was with Barnard Bensen LLP. Although you had been hired to pursue a CA, you had decided after a week that your preference was for enterprise business systems technology and strategic financial management. Consequently, you obtained your CMA designation, and sought all possible enterprise business systems technology assignments, especially those involving front end, customer-facing applications such as customer relationship management (CRM). Now you are a manager at Barnard Bensen in the customer solutions practice.

Customer-Facing Applications

CRM systems and other respective software allow organizations to automate and increase the efficiency of their front offices. The front office deals with an organization's acquisition and retention of, and interaction and personalized transactions with, customers, as opposed to the back office or the behind-the-scenes systems that deal with production, logistics, administration, and accounting powered by enterprise resource planning systems such as PeopleSoft and SAP. Customer-facing applications ensure that staff on the front lines have easy access to customer histories, interactions, and transactions. They also provide for customer self-service capabilities through interactive voice, data and Internet channels. Specialist CRM software links together all of these parts of the business and allows staff at all levels of the organization to see up-to-the-second customer information on a continuous basis.

A customer database or more precisely a data warehouse is utilized to implement CRM systems. Data warehouses contain all customer information to support real-time analyses that assist in managing the customer relationship at all touch points or points of interaction with customers — Web, telephone, e-mail, and face-to-face, plus point-of-sale, billing, or other operational systems — both inbound and outbound. CRM makes sure that customers are treated the same, regardless of how they are interacting with the organization. For example, if a customer contacts a call centre with a service complaint, the call-centre representative can see that the customer has a large order pending and expedite the service to keep the customer content. In this way, CRM is called database marketing.

Specifically, the CRM data warehouse contains details on customers, names, addresses, when and what they have purchased, when and why have they contacted the organization, how they have responded to advertisements and promotions, etc. A data warehouse should have all information on all customers, and ideally it should maintain information on prospective customers as well as past customers.

CRMs are important for three reasons. First, customers are an organization's most valuable asset. Each customer on the list is expensive and time-consuming to acquire. Past customers are the most likely to be future customers. Second, most organizations do a poor job of dealing with customers. This is usually because the organization is unable to coordinate all of its customer touch points. Third, the Internet and information technology allow for a much greater proportion of customer interactions to be captured, coordinated, and delivered digitally.

Amazon.com provides an example of an organization using a CRM system. Amazon users browse the Web site, then order books and CDs using formatted Web pages by filling in order, personal, and credit card details. Amazon's system captures all of this data, using it to push recommendations based on customers buying histories. Customer files are used to automatically send e-mails on the status of orders, and to mass-market new service like auctions. Furthermore, if customers are browsing travel books on, for example, Jamaica, Amazon's system can flash up a recommendation for a Bob Marley CD, with one-click ordering. Moreover, Amazon has a complete record of a customer e-mails and its own responses. Amazon also collects data on which promotions work and which do not.

Siebel and Clarify are two CRM software systems. Each of these systems allows organizations to collect and analyze customer data and in some cases initiate real-time responses. Older CRM software packages or operational applications are limited to gathering data from customer interactions such as service calls, sales transactions, and Web site activity. The newer CRM software packages include analytical applications which evaluate customer data for patterns that assist with the development of marketing campaigns and targeted sales pitches. CRM systems are able to integrate all touch points, whether telephone, Internet, or personally initiated. Information for the latter is the most difficult to capture, as it often is manually inputted.

Banks are using CRM systems to restore personalization into the banking relationship. Twenty-five years ago banking was personal, face-to-face, and largely conducted in the branch. Then through the introduction of cost-reducing automatic teller machine (ATM) technology, customer closeness was lost. Banks were able to further reduce costs by automating more transactions, but at the cost of being detached from customers. Banks use CRM technology to efficiently and effectively understand customer requirements and to respond to problems. However, banks need to be careful that the CRMs are not used primarily for cross selling other bank services.

Request for Proposal

You are the manager assigned to write the proposal for implementing a CRM (customer relationship management) system at Yoour University, the major university in the capital city where you live. You learn from the partner in charge of the information technology practice that the request for proposals (RFP) has come from Yoour University's president who sees a need to change the way students and the university interact with administrative matters. In the RFP, there are three reasons underlying the president's desire for a CRM system. First, a CRM would reduce costs from the multitude of overlapping and expensive systems that provide an incomplete service to students. Data from organizations such as Dell citing costs per customer service interaction as $10 with personal contact, $7.50 with call centres, $2.45 with voice response systems, and $0.18 with Internet have influenced the president in her desire for a CRM system. Second, a CRM system would provide students with improved services by having a coordinated focus to their inquiries and transac-

tions with the university. Third, improvements in the student experience would instill positive feelings, thereby lead them to be better donors after they graduate and become alumni members. In effect, the president wants a description of what will be subject to a CRM system. With that description, the president can contact CRM vendors for quotations for an installed CRM system

At a meeting arranged by the president to provide information to consulting organizations interested in submitting proposals, you learn that Yoour University has 35,000 undergraduate students and 10,000 graduate students. Back office activities are handled by an enterprise resource planning system by PeopleSoft. For the front office activities dealing with students and the focus of CRM, Yoour University has the following computerized or manual systems.

1. Admissions. The Admissions unit is responsible for obtaining enrolments. This is done by recording all applicants and then based on established criteria accepting those who qualify. This responsibility also involves communications with applicants by mail, telephone, and e-mail. It also assigns accepted students with unique identifying numbers. Manual forms are used with the admissions process.

2. Registrar. This unit keeps track of student academic progress with what is called the student information system. It records all grades, grade changes, reactivations, faculty transfers, course adds, course drops, etc. It interacts with students using the voice response system, the Web page, e-mail, surface mail, and telephone. The registrar unit also does a program audit once students have declared they expect to graduate, which is either at the spring or fall convocation.

One shortcoming was noted; the student information system does not do prerequisite checks to ensure that students have the proper background for the courses they are taking. Also, a new Web site was launched to bring under one umbrella all existing interactive services for students. These services include not only the capacity to change an address or SIN, but also to view grades and student accounts.

Presently, the admissions unit and the registrar's unit are located in separate buildings across campus from each other. There are plans to place both under the same roof to improve services to students.

3. Transcripts. Current and past students contact the registrar's unit for certified copies of their transcripts. Name and address information is not used to update student or alumni records.

4. Financial assistance. This unit has primary responsibility for all aspects of a student's financial relationship with the university, including administration of provincial assistance, allocation of bursaries and scholarships, and the collection of fees. There are a number of systems involved. Recently, this unit developed a new student account statement and made it available on the Web. It also implemented Internet and telephone banking to make it easier for students to make their payments to the university without having to wait in a lineup.

5. Residence. Each student in residence is recorded in the residence system. The data collected includes name, home address, next of kin in case of emergency, and room/apartment assignment. Also, there is a system that looks after recording the payment of various residence fees.

6. Faculty. Each faculty, such as Arts, Education, and Business, answers questions posed by students regarding their programs or courses, required electives, location of classes, dates for final examinations, etc. Generally this is done by a specialized unit, commonly called the office of student assistance and services. Students also contact the dean, associate dean or an administrative person on these matters. Some faculties have, on their own, established Web pages to proactively address student questions and concerns.

7. Departments. Each department has administrative personnel who answer questions posed by students regarding their program or courses required, electives, location of classes, dates for final examinations, submission of assign-

ments, etc. To be proactive, some departments have established Web pages to address student questions and concerns.

8. Alumni. Once students graduate they automatically become members of the Yoour University alumni. Although the names of all graduates are correctly recorded along with the degree or degrees, the addresses have not been accurately maintained. A few years ago, an organization was allowed to contact or more often attempt to contact all possible alumni in order to compile an alumni directory. The company was allowed to sell the directory. Yoour University benefited from up-to-date addresses for many alumni members. However, at the termination of the project, addresses were listed for only about half of the graduates, and many of those addresses were incorrect. Other than this arrangement, Yoour University has not before or after attempted to systematically keep track of its alumni members. It is estimated that only 35 percent of the addresses are correct.

9. Advancement. Fundraising is done or at least coordinated by the Advancement unit. Careful records are maintained of all donors. This list is used for regular fundraising activities, with the argument that the best donors are those who have donated in the past.

10. Library. A separate record is maintained of all persons with library cards. This list is automatically updated with changes in the status of students, faculty, or staff. Alumni members are allowed to obtain library privileges at a nominal annual change.

Required In order to prepare a proposal for designing an effective CRM system or systems, identify the existing systems and document what they do. Then design for Yoour University a CRM system or systems to address what should be done.

SECTION III

Activity Costing Cases

Benevolent and Research Society

The mission of the Benevolent and Research Society is to eradicate a certain prevalent disease and in the meantime enhance the quality of life for people living with it. This is done by delivering educational and patient programs, and by participating in research, fundraising and advocacy. Volunteers and paid employees share these responsibilities.

The Society has a national office and 10 divisions across Canada. Substantial importance is placed on research coordinated by the national research institute, which receives 48 percent of the revenues. These revenues come from public fundraising. None comes from government organizations.

The subject division has 54 employees. Employees and volunteers at this office coordinate provincial activities, prepare and develop programs for use by the districts, units, and branches. This project focuses on the activities of the eight employees in the division's accounting department, which also provides accounting services for the districts and units. The department is vital to the continued operation of the organization because it processes accounts receivable, accounts payable, cheques, etc. and produces current, accurate financial information. This information assists all levels of the division to plan, control, and make decisions.

POSITIONS AND ACTIVITIES

Listed below are the positions in the accounting department and some major duties assigned to each.

Accounting Supervisor

- Hires, trains, supervises, motivates, and evaluates departmental staff

- Oversees the operation of the accounts payable and revenue sections
- Prepares monthly financial statements
- Reviews, verifies, and coordinates the preparation of budgets across the province
- Ensures funds are invested in approved financial institutions at high yields
- Checks authorizations on all requests for payment
- Works with the auditors to ensure an accurate and efficient external audit
- Verifies all transactions before entering into the general ledger

Assistant Accounting Supervisor

- Reconciles cash accounts and bank statements for the units against the division's ledger
- Monitors and provides day-to-day direction to the other accounting staff and accounting support to staff in district and unit offices
- Analyzes various accounts on the computer and provides written reports as required
- Maintains and posts the designated bequest ledger monthly, encodes and checks accuracy of account numbers
- Reviews and redirects daily mail
- Obtains investment rates and makes investments

Senior Accounting Clerk

- Prepares monthly bank reconciliations for the general transfer accounts, units' working funds, and transfer accounts
- Reconciles the unit and branch imprest, petty cash, employee, temporary, and unit advances with the general ledger

Adapted from a case by Paul Ahima, Michael Appiah, Mark Dalrymple, Yvonne Cheng, Manjit Rai, Paulett Ramsey and Sonia Shkolnik.

- Records daily the revenue reports and bank statements for all units
- Maintains petty cash float at specified levels
- Records the mileage and gas used and prepares annual gas tax rebate submission forms
- Prepares reports, conducts account analysis, acts as backup to assistant accounting supervisor and in-memorial-receipts clerk

Senior Accounts Payable Clerk

- Verifies accuracy of vendor invoices and reconciles them with monthly statements
- Codes and keys in invoices for payment, produces cheques and the cheque register bi-weekly
- Responds to suppliers' and units' queries and maintains up-to-date vendor files
- Obtains signatures on cheques, mails or distributes cheques
- Relieves receptionist

Junior Accounts Payable Clerk

- Records receipts of units' reimbursement claims, verifies vouchers to cheque copies, assigns accounts to various charges; checks for adjustments to the working fund from bank reconciliation
- Checks unit reimbursements to ensure adherence to policy and accuracy of account numbers
- Keys invoices, unit reimbursements into the computer for the production of cheques
- Separates cheques, sends to payees, sorts and files copies
- Annually removes appropriate files for microfilming or storing and prepares files for next fiscal year
- Relieves receptionist

In-Memorial-Receipts Clerk

- Receives and verifies balanced daily control sheets itemizing details, cheques and cash from assistant accounting supervisor; classifies and credits funds to appropriate accounts
- Prepares deposit slips and makes daily deposits
- Issues and sends donations and bequest receipts and in-memorial cards
- Prepares accounts receivable invoices upon request
- Receives and processes patient transportation reimbursement claims for all units

- Types correspondence and bequest statement
- Relieves receptionist

Data Entry Clerk

- Keys in all transactions to the general ledger
- Collates and prepares monthly statements to all units
- Files source documents
- Maintains the receipt book control sheets by assigning receipt book numbers to units and updating same
- Keys in annual budgets for all departments, districts and units

Receptionist

- Provides empathetic and courteous telephone and reception services to callers and visitors
- Arranges for taxis and limousine services
- Provides word processing for the accounting supervisor
- Enters imprest reimbursements into the computer
- Verifies outgoing cheques

Instead of listing activities by employee, the following schedule groups common activities.

1. Hires, motivates and evaluates departmental staff

2. Trains, supervises and oversees employees' daily activities
   - oversees daily activities of department
   - checks invoices and outgoing cheques
   - checks investment vehicles
   - checks petty cash transactions

3. Processes invoices and reimbursement claims
   - receives invoices and reimbursement claims
   - sends to appropriate department for authorization
   - codes invoices
   - keys in data

4. Prepares cheques from computerized information
   - issues cheques
   - attaches backup information to cheques
   - checks the accuracy of the cheques
   - obtains signatures on cheques
   - separates, sorts and files cheque copies
   - forwards cheques to payees or requisitioner

5. Processing revenues
   - receives donations, bequests, and in-memorial revenues

EXHIBIT 1

	AS	AAS	SAC	SAPC	JAPC	IMRC	DEC	R
Training and supervising	X	X		X				
Processing invoices and reimbursement claims				X	X	X		
Prepares cheques	X	X		X	X	X	X	X
Prepares monthly financial statements	X	X	X	X	X	X	X	X
Coordination and re-distribution of budgets	X						X	
Telephone and reception services				X	X	X	X	
Accounts receivable invoices	X			X				
Processing revenues and making deposits		X	X			X		
Obtains investment rates and makes investments	X	X						
Reconciles all accounts	X	X	X	X				
General ledger entries		X	X	X				

Note: AS — accounting supervisor; AAS — assistant accounting supervisor; SAC — senior accounting clerk; SAPC — senior accounts payable clerk; DEC — data entry clerk; JAPC — junior accounts payable clerk; R — receptionist; and IMRC — in-memorial-receipts clerk.

- prepares deposit list
- checks deposit list
- makes deposit

6. Reconciliation of accounts
   - keys in all revenues to general ledger
   - reconciles cash flow and bank statements
   - reconciles working fund and transfer accounts
   - reconciles various advances and petty cash float

7. Prepares accounts receivable invoices
   - receives request to issue invoice for patient transportation, overpayment of expense claims or non-chargeable expenses
   - codes and inputs data into the computer
   - prints invoices
   - verifies accuracy and mails invoices

8. Budgeting
   - prepares budget forms
   - submits to division, districts and units
   - reviews and verifies budget submissions
   - keys in budget data
   - prints and distributes individual budgets

9. Reception
   - responds to incoming telephone calls and greets visitors

- provides word processing services to supervisor
- arranges for taxi and limousine services

ACTIVITY MATRIX

The matrix in Exhibit 1 displays the relationship between major activities and positions in the accounting department.

Cross training and scheduling are not obvious in the lists of major duties. However, there is a system in place under which employees can do more than their own jobs to ensure ongoing activities during periods of vacation or illness.

OBSERVATIONS

Observations and interviews determined the actual time spent on each activity. The table in Exhibit 2 shows these times.

ACTIVITY CHANGES

Volunteers perform many activities at the districts and units. One activity change would be to have district and unit staff check, approve, and accept responsibility for all reports, invoices, purchase orders, expense claims, budgets, and reimbursement

EXHIBIT 2

Activities	Actual Time Requirements	
Supervising	5	minutes an employee a day
Obtains investment rates	5	minutes a telephone call (3 calls per investment)
Makes investment	10	minutes per investment
Issues petty cash	2	minutes per issue
Checks an invoice	1	minutes per invoice
Sends invoice for authorization	0.5	minutes per invoice
Manually codes invoice	0.25	minutes per invoice
Keys in cheque information	1.5	minutes per invoice
Manually types comments on cheque	1	minute per cheque
Matches cheque with invoice	30	seconds per invoice
Separates cheques	15	seconds per cheque
Files cheque copy	15	seconds per cheque copy
Checks unit reimbursement claim	5	minutes per claim
Prepares daily deposit list	2	hours per list
Makes deposit at bank	1	hour per deposit
Types receipt/in memorial card	5	minutes per receipt/card
Keys in transaction to general ledger	2	minutes per transaction
Reconciles cash	45	minutes a reconciliation
Reconciles bank statement	45	minutes per statement
Prepares monthly financial statement	30	hours per month
Keys in budget data	10	minutes per budget
Distributes individual budget	1	minute per budget
Prepares annual audited financial statements	60	hours per year
Responds to incoming telephone calls	0.5	minute per call

claims. This checking would reduce errors. This would lead to savings: approximately 0.12 seconds per invoice; and a 20 percent decrease for checking reports, purchase orders, expense claims, budgets, and reimbursement claims.

A second change would be to purchase minor computer software to list outstanding cheques at the end of the month. Specifically, these changes would allow the printing of receipts, cards, and comment lines on cheques. The savings would be five hours a month for bank statement reconciliations, one minute per cheque, and approximately two minutes per receipt or card.

Third, send mail directly from the mailroom to the incurring department for authorization and general ledger account coding. Then submit to the accounting department for payment. This would save 0.5 minutes per invoice.

ESTABLISH STANDARDS

The accounting department has the following response standards:

- respond to inquiries within two days,
- pay suppliers within 14 days or 30 days (decided by distance from the division office),
- reimburse units within 14 days, and
- make daily deposits by 3:00 p.m.

With these response standards, time-to-complete-an-activity standards were developed (see Exhibit 3).

The standards for the other activities remain at the observed rates.

ACTIVITY DRIVERS

Historical volume data with differences during the day, week and year were not readily available. Thus, the team questioned each member of the department regarding cyclical patterns during the day, week, month and year. Although activities levels did vary, there were opportunities to smooth or manage these fluctuations.

Notable increases in workload occur during the April campaign, where the accounting department

EXHIBIT 3

Activities	Standard Time Requirements	
Matches cheque with invoice	25	seconds per invoice
Separates cheques	10	seconds per cheque
Files cheque copy	10	seconds per cheque copy
Checks unit reimbursement claim	3.5	minutes per claim
Prepares daily deposit list	1.5	hours per list
Types receipt or in-memorial card	4	minutes per receipt/card
Keys in transaction to general ledger	1.5	minutes a transaction
Reconciles cash flow	30	minutes per unit reconciliation
Reconciles bank statement	30	minutes per statement
Prepares monthly financial statements	27	hours per month
Keys in budget data	8	minutes per budget
Distributes individual budget	1	minute per budget
Prepares annual audited financial statements	55	hours per year

EXHIBIT 4

Activities	Regular Volume		Campaign Volume	
Invoices, expense claims processed	40	per day	40	per day
Cheques	130	per week	130	per week
Receipts	20	per day	25	per day
In memorial cards	10	per day	13	per day
Data entries to general ledger	750	per day	937	per day
Incoming cheques per deposit	25	per day	31	per day
Incoming telephone calls	400	per day	500	per day
Coordinate budgets	140	per year	140	per year

experiences an approximately 25 percent increase in the number of donations. Exhibit 4 illustrates the increases, which can be managed by smoothing or shifting the work to later time periods.

EMPLOYEE HOUR REQUIREMENTS

Exhibit 5 identifies the volume of the activity driver per average day, the standard time for the activity, and their product the required employee time per activity. Accumulating by position and comparing to the available employee time per day, yields the utilization rate.

Utilization specifies the proportion of occupied employee hours if he or she accomplishes the activities within the established time standards. A full working day contains 8 working hours. That

time decreases by 15 percent for lunches and other breaks. Expected total hours available for work 6.8 hours per employee. This would be 100 percent utilization, but 85 to 90 percent would be a more reasonable expectation.

SCHEDULING EMPLOYEES

The utilization rates suggest eliminating the assistant accounting supervisor and junior accounts payable clerk positions, and reassign their activities to other positions.

The assistant accounting supervisor and junior accounts payable clerk work at utilization rates of 43 percent and 51 percent, respectively. The activities of the first position overlap those of the accounting supervisor and senior accounting clerk.

EXHIBIT 5: EMPLOYEE HOUR REQUIREMENTS

	Volume	Standard Time		Per Day Required Employee Minutes
Accounting Supervisor				
Hires, trains (yearly)	1	15	hours	4
Oversees the operation of accounts payable and revenue sections minutes per day per employee	7	5	minutes	35
Prepares monthly financial statements (monthly)	1	27	hours	81
Reviews and coordinates all budgets (yearly)	1	68	hours	17
Makes investments (daily)	2	5	minutes	10
Checks authorizations on all requests for payment (daily)	40	1	minute	40
Works with the auditors (yearly)	1	55	hours	14
Verifies transactions (daily)	1	30	minutes	30
Utilization rate, 56 percent				230
Assistant Accounting Supervisor				
Reconciles bank statements (monthly)	60	30	minutes	90
Monitors and provides day-to-day accounting direction (daily)	7	5	minutes	35
Analyzes accounts (daily)	2	5	minutes	10
Maintains and posts designated bequest ledger monthly, codes and checks account numbers (monthly)	40	5	minutes	10
Reviews and redirects mail (daily)	20	1	minute	20
Makes investments (daily)	2	5	minutes	10
Utilization rate, 43 percent				175
Senior Accounting Clerk				
Reconciles bank statements (monthly)	60	30	minutes	90
Reconciles other accounts with general ledger (monthly)	60	30	minutes	90
Records transactions (monthly)	60	30	minutes	90
Maintains petty cash float (daily)	2	2	minutes	4
Records the mileage and gas (monthly)	20	5	minutes	5
Prepares reports and conducts account analysis, backup to assistant accounting supervisor and in-memorial-receipts clerk (daily)	1	10	minutes	10
Utilization rate, 71 percent				289
Senior Accounts Payable Clerk				
Verifies vendor invoices, reconciles with monthly statements (daily)	40	1	minute	40
Codes, keys in invoices for payment, produces cheques and cheque register (daily)	26	5	minutes	130
Responds to queries and maintains vendor files (daily)	10	2	minutes	20
Obtains signatures on cheques, mails or distributes cheques (daily)	26	2	minutes	52
Relieves receptionist (daily)	1	30	minutes	30
Utilization rate, 67 percent				272
Junior Accounts Payable Clerk				
Records unit reimbursement claims, assigns accounts and checks working fund accounts (daily)	6	5	minutes	30
Checks unit reimbursements for adherence to policy (daily)	6	5	minutes	30
Keys in invoices, unit reimbursements (daily)	60	1	minute	60
Prepares cheques for distribution and files copies (daily)	26	1	minute	26
Replace files, microfilming (daily)	1	6	minutes	6
Relieves receptionist (daily)	1	60	minutes	60
Utilization rate, 51 percent				212

	Volume	Standard Time		Per Day Required Employee Minutes
In-Memorial-Receipts Clerk				
Receives and verifies balanced daily control sheets, classifies, credits funds to accounts, prepares deposit slips, and makes deposits (daily)	1	180	minutes	180
Issues donation and bequest receipts and in-memorial cards (weekly)	30	4	minutes	120
Prepares accounts receivable invoices (daily)	2	5	minutes	10
Receives, processes patient transportation reimbursement claims for units (daily)	6	3	minutes	18
Types correspondence (daily)	1	30	minutes	30
Relieves receptionist (daily)	1	30	minutes	30
Utilization rate, 95 percent				388
Data Entry Clerk				
Keys in transactions to general ledger (daily)	200	1.5	minutes	300
Collates monthly statements (daily)	6	0.5	minutes	3
Files source documents (daily)	30	0.5	minutes	15
Maintains the receipt book control sheets by assigning receipt book numbers to units, updating (daily)	2	2.5	minutes	5
Keys in annual budgets (yearly)	140	10	minutes	6
Utilization rate, 81 percent				329
Receptionist				
Provides telephone and reception services to callers, visitors (daily)	400	0.5	minutes	200
Arranges for taxis and limousines (daily)	2	2	minutes	4
Provides word processing services (daily)	1	60	minutes	60
Enters imprest reimbursements (daily)	6	5	minutes	30
Verifies outgoing cheques (daily)	26	1	minute	26
Utilization rate, 78 percent				320

The senior accounting clerk could undertake the first position's bank reconciliation and account analysis activities. Moreover, the accounting supervisor and the assistant accounting supervisor could provide the day-to-day accounting direction to districts and units. Account number coding and accuracy checking are part of the duties of the senior accounts payable clerk. The receptionist can redirect daily mail. Also, the senior accounts payable clerk should post and maintain the bequest ledger.

The junior accounts payable clerk's activities can be distributed as follows:

- Verify unit reimbursements — senior accounts payable clerk

- Input invoices and reimbursements — senior accounts payable clerk, data entry clerk and/or receptionist

- Run cheques, verify and type comments from adjustment book — senior accounts payable clerk

- Filing and annual file changeover — senior accounts clerk or data entry clerk

The elimination of these positions will result in cost savings and the removal of the friction that comes from ill-defined and overlapping positions.

INFORMATION SYSTEM

On an annual, monthly, and daily basis, an information system would include expected volumes for activity drivers, such as number of invoices, cheques issued, budgets prepared, etc. The occupants of the positions have responsibility for accomplishing the volumes, along with the time standards for accomplishing each activity. There would also be a targeted utilization rate with these assignments. This part of the information system is similar to a budget. However, instead of dollar amounts, it would be in terms of expected number of activities to be done and standard times per activity.

Actual volumes for activity drivers would be compared to expected volumes, and variances would be analyzed. The learning from the feedback would help in maintaining currently attainable standards and accuracy in forecasting activity driver volumes.

Required Comment on how this completed case followed the project requirements, especially in the development of activity drivers.

Blackjack

Blackjack is a gambling game offered by a casino along with wheel of fortune and roulette. The casino operates during the 10 days of a city's annual exhibition. The casino distributes profits among charitable organizations. Readers unfamiliar with blackjack may want to consult Exhibit 1.

The blackjack operation consists of five positions as noted in the following diagram. This study's concern is with the dealers.

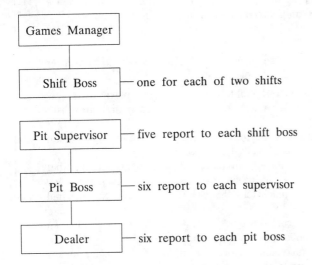

A games manager is responsible for blackjack and the other two games. There is one shift boss for each of the two shifts (10 a.m. to 6 p.m. and 6 p.m. to 2 a.m.). Each pit supervisor is responsible for six pit bosses, and each pit boss supervises all activities, players, and dealers at six tables. Dealers are responsible for their immediate table.

Each dealer works an eight-hour shift. After an hour of work, there is a 15-minute break. Thus, a pit of 30 tables requires 36 dealers. A dealer's responsibilities include: sell chips to players for cash, monitor player activity for unlawful behaviour, make no assumptions on players' hands, make sure players intentions to either hit or pass are made clearly, and report any irregularities or errors to the pit boss.

Activities

Two groups classify dealer activities. The first are direct activities. These consist of dealing the cards, shuffling the cards, and exchanging money and chips. Dealing the cards is the actual playing of the game. Exhibit 1 describes these activities. The actions involved are dealing out the cards, paying out winnings, and collecting lost bets. Shuffling the cards consists of the dealer calling out "shuffle up" to the pit boss, and pausing briefly for acknowledgement. The dealer then mixes the cards using a series of well-defined movements. A final direct activity is that of making change. Here the dealer accepts money in exchange for chips or for an equal amount in different denominations.

The second are indirect activities, non-essential to blackjack, but which enhance the flow of the game. They are organizing the chip tray, conversing, and shift changes. The first is done to make money changing smoother and quicker. Conversing can be broken down into two types: to enhance customer relations, and to answer questions and explain the game. As for breaks, they are vital for maintaining dealer performance and customer satisfaction. Exhibit 2 shows these activities.

Dealer activities had few opportunities for improvement. More opportunities existed from improved matching of dealers and players. The differences in skills place a dealer in one of three categories:

Neophyte: They started training only two months before the casino opened. The games manager estimated that 30 percent of the dealers were of this type.

Adapted from a case by J. Herschmiller, B. Wong and W. Yung.

EXHIBIT 1: BLACKJACK RULES OF PLAY

General Description

Blackjack is a card game played with a pack of four standard decks dealt from a shoe by a dealer in which up to seven players participate. Only the dealer may touch the cards, which he plays face up.

Object of Game

Each player attempts to achieve a higher total point value per hand than the dealer, without exceeding a value of 21. If a point count exceeds 21, the hand has "busted" and the bet is automatically lost. If the player's and dealer's point totals are equal, this is a "push" (stand-off) and nobody wins or loses.

Point Value of Cards

There are rules for counting points:

- Aces count "1" or "11" at the player's election. Face cards count "10," all other cards represent their face value. Card suits do not count.
- A "soft" hand is one that contains an ace counted as 11. All other hands are "hard" in point value. A "hard" hand contains no aces or the aces counted as "1."

Natural or Blackjack

If the first two cards dealt to a player total 21, this is a "natural "or "Blackjack" and takes precedence over any three-or-more card point total of 21. If player and dealer have a blackjack, it is a "push."

Player Options

Each player receives one card, then the dealer takes one card. The players then receive a second card after which each player has the following options:

- *Hit:* Receives an additional card (a blackjack cannot be hit). To obtain the card, the player makes a beckoning motion with his hand. After each "hit" the player may continue to hit as many cards as he wishes until his/her point count reaches or exceeds 21.
- *Stand:* Receive no additional cards. The player signals the dealer by waving his hand, open palm down. Players use only hand signals. Dealers will not accept verbal decisions.
- *Double down:* If first two cards dealt total 10 or 11, the player can place an additional, separate bet equal to the original. It is placed in the square. Then one additional card is received. A player may not double down on a blackjack. If the dealer makes a blackjack, the player loses only the original bet.
- *Pair splitting:* If first two cards are of equal point value, each becomes a separate hand by placing an additional, separate bet equal to the original. It is placed on the outside lines. Only split aces are limited to one additional card per hand. The player plays one hand before the other. If the dealer makes a blackjack, the player loses only the original bet. A two-card 21 on a split hand is not a blackjack for the purposes of a payoff. When splitting any pair, no more than two hands may develop from the original two cards.

Betting and Limits

There are rules for betting.

- Betting is done only with chips purchased from a dealer.
- Chips of different value have different colours. The chip value and colour of each denomination are noted:

$ 0.50	bronze
$ 1.00	red
$ 5.00	black
$ 25.00	blue and yellow
$100.00	brown, red, and gold

- The dealer's chip tray is arranged, going from left to right in the following sequence: $1.00, $5.00, $25.00, $100.00 (if applicable), $25.00, $5.00, $1.00, $0.50.
- Bets are valid only when put upon the space provided on the table before dealing commences. They remain unchanged during play (unless splitting or doubling down). Chips outside the betting square are not considered bets.

- Unalterable betting limits shall be:

$2–$50 Tables	=	one hand	$2–50		
		two hands	$20–50	per hand	
		three hands	$50	per hand	
$5–$100 Tables	=	one hand	$5–100		
		two hands	$40–100	per hand	
		three hands	$100	per hand	

- Bets shall be of $1 multiples.
- Players shall not play, or exercise any form of control over more than three betting spaces.

Pay-offs

Players with blackjacks get paid at three to two; other winning hands get paid at one to one.

Sequence of Play

There are some basic steps to blackjack:

1. *Cards.* The dealer deals cards from a pack of 208 new cards (four decks). They are "ribbon" spread on the table for front and back examination by the dealer. There are no jokers. They remain ribbon spread, face up, until play commences. Shuffling is always done twice.

    Dealers change cards at the shuffle. Pit bosses remove used cards from the table. Simultaneously they check for flaws, bind the cards with a rubber band, and record with an attached note the date, time of day and game number. The pit boss signs a note certifying that cards are free of flaws, or shall report flaws immediately to the games manager. The same procedure applies at the close of the final day.

    If the game is temporarily closed and the dealer is relieved without replacement, the pit boss removes the shoe and cards for safekeeping. If all players leave, the dealer combines the cards from the shoe with discards, ribbon spreads them face-up on the table, awaiting commencement of play. The general manager collects all cards at the final day closing. He retains them for at least seven days.

2. *Shuffle, cut, or stop card.* Before play commences, the dealer thoroughly shuffles the cards, and calls to the pit boss, "shuffle up" and pauses briefly for acknowledgement. The dealer uses only the table ribbon-shuffle, with all cards face-down and none exposed to anyone.

    To start, the dealer moves the pack forward on the table and cuts it into two approximate halves. Then the dealer cuts each to make four similarly sized piles of cards. The piles are then shuffled according to a standard procedure.

    After shuffling, the dealer squares the centre pile of all four decks. A player cuts by inserting a cut-card. The player's card must be at least one deck deep. If it should occur that no player wants to make the cut, the dealer cuts. The dealer then places the front section of cut pack, with cut-card, behind the rest of pack. Next, the dealer squares the cards against the shoe and inserts the cut-card 35 to 55 cards from bottom of pack before placing the cards in the shoe. After placing in the shoe, the first card is kept face down, i.e., "burned." Burning is the placement of a card face down in the discard holder. The dealer does not show the burned card.

    When the stop-card appears during play, the dealer shuffles the pack after completing the current rough, no matter the number of cards left in the shoe. Then the dealer removes the remaining cards in the shoe, and places them in front of the chip tray for reshuffling.

3. *Basic play.* The deal begins when all players have made their wagers within the betting squares. The dealer runs his hand over the table from right to left to check all bets.

    Starting on the left, the dealer gives each player one card face up. The dealer also takes one face-up card. Then the dealer gives the players a second face-up card. Players receive hits by a hand signal (motion towards themselves). Similarly, players show their intentions to not take a hit with hand signals (motion away from themselves).

4. *Change-ins.* Dealers do not accept cash or chips from players by hand. Players place chips on table for pickup by dealer.

    Dealers call out all colour and money changes by stating the amount.

5. *Tray management.* Dealers keep their trays neat, especially before shuffling.

6. *Fills.* As a tray gets low on chips, the pit boss orders the dealer a fill. This is a tray of chips totalling $3,575, of a distinctive chip arrangement. Both the dealer and the pit boss will check the amount and sign a statement confirming it.

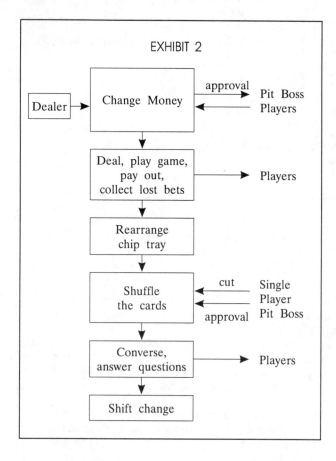

EXHIBIT 2

The above data on player categories and spending can be explained in terms of money spent per hour, as noted below:

	Time Spent	Money Spent	Money Spent per Hour
Fun-Seeker	2 hrs	$ 20.00	$10.00
Rambo	4 hrs	200.00	50.00
Regular	8 hrs	30.00	3.75

The pit boss divides the tables into two types: high limit ($5 to $100 bets), and low limit ($2 to $50 bets). The games manager estimated the relative proportion of the three types of players at both the high- and low-limit tables to be:

	High-Limit Table	Low-Limit Table
Fun-Seeker	1	2
Rambo	5	2
Regular	1	3

Note, full tables have seven players.

The following table converts the amount of money spent in an hour into the amount spent in a round. There are about 41 rounds per hour of dealing. A round is completed when the dealer deals a complete game to each player. The table shows what each type of player loses after each hand.

	Spent Per Hour	Spent Per Round
Fun-Seeker	$10.00	$0.24
Rambo	50.00	1.22
Regular	3.75	0.09

Then, the next table uses the above numbers to construct an expected revenue schedule. It considers the number and type of players at each table.

	High-Limit Table		Low-Limit Table	
Fun-Seeker	0.24	(1)*	0.48	(2)
Rambo	6.10	(5)	2.44	(2)
Regular	0.09	(1)	0.27	(3)
Expected Revenue	$6.43		$3.19	

* The brackets show the numbers of players.

Note, the expected revenue per round remains constant despite the speed of the dealer. The goal, then, for management is to maximize the total number of rounds that a player goes through. Since rambos drop the most per round, management should strive to get them through as many rounds of blackjack games as possible. As high-

Intermediate: These were dealers who had dealt at a regular casino within the last year. Many of these dealers were neophytes last year. About 30 percent of the dealers were intermediates.

Expert: These dealers were full-time blackjack dealers for longer than 18 months. About 40 percent of the dealers were experts.

Similarly, according to their skill and likelihood to spend money, players were categorized into three types:

Fun-Seeker: These players typically are there for the exhibition and merely want to try gambling. They are often first-timers and usually stay about two hours. They usually play conservatively and will lose $20 each on average.

Rambo: They know how to play blackjack and come for recreation. These players do not care if they lose. They come for fun. Rambos stay for about four hours and tend to lose about $200 per sitting.

Regular: These retired persons appear daily at casinos. Regulars tend to stay "rooted" for approximately eight hours on average and lose about $30 each time.

limit tables possess most of the rambos, a high-limit table's expected revenues more than double the expected revenues from a low-limit table. Thus, management should staff these tables with the more proficient dealers.

Neophytes comprise 30 percent of the total dealer population, and experts and intermediates represent 40 percent and 30 percent, respectively. Therefore, of the 36 dealers employed in a single pit, 11 would be neophytes, 11 intermediates, and 14 experts. With a pit having 30 tables (15 high-limit and 15 low-limit), staffing should entail attempting to fill all high limit tables with experts and intermediates if needed. Fill all low-limit tables with neophytes. Thus:

	High-Limit Tables	Low-Limit Tables	Totals
Neophytes	0	11	11
Intermediates	4	7	11
Experts	14	0	14
Totals	18	18	36

Observations

The data came from observing dealers for several hours. Observations included:

- time to complete a shoe, i.e., 208 cards,
- number of deals per shoe,
- time to shuffle,
- time to change money,
- time to rearrange the chip tray,
- time that the dealer was involved in conversation with players, and
- time that the dealer was involved in conversation with pit bosses.

Data from the observations were incorporated into activity section.

Activity Changes

The government regulates and standardizes dealer actions. Thus, no changes to the "dealing" process were possible. One idea was to mechanize certain aspects of the process (i.e., automating the shuffle). The games manager quickly dashed this idea saying that players mistrust any kind of machine involvement in a card game. However, two opportunities exist for improving the performance of activities. First, divide the dealers into neophyte, intermediate and expert. This categorization enables appropriate work assignments and training. Second, categorize players as fun-seekers, rambo, and regular. These categorizations enable optimal assignment of dealers to players to maximize profits.

Standard times came from a combination of observations, activity changes, and interviews with managers and dealers. Exhibit 3 shows these standards. More importantly, the following table shows the standard number of deals per hour.

	Deals Per Hour	Rounds Per Hour
Neophyte	220	31
Intermediate	278	40
Expert	371	53

These standards apply to seven players at a table. They can be prorated for fewer players.

Activity Drivers

The number of players would be the activity driver. However, there was no historical data. This did not detract from the proposed improvements. The recommended changes apply to all activity levels.

Scheduling

Interviews with several pit bosses revealed that staffing was a totally random process. That is, a dealer's relative experience did not influence table assignment. Any table took any dealer. Thus, an "average dealer" method of staffing existed.

A two step calculation is needed to estimate the revenue from this method of staffing. First, determine the number of rounds dealt per hour per table, namely:

0.3 [neophyte] × 31 rounds per hour

+ 0.3 [intermediate] × 40 rounds per hour

+ 0.4 [expert] × 53 rounds per hour

= 42.5 rounds per hour

Second, multiply the yields per round by the rounds per hour:

High-Limit Tables	Low-Limit Tables
$6.43 per round	$3.19 per round
× 42.5 rounds per hour	× 42.5 rounds per hour
= $273.28 per hour	= $135.58 per hour

The total revenue for the present staffing method, with 15 high-limit and 15 low-limit tables, is $6,132.90 per hour.

In contrast to the average dealer model, the recommended method would produce more as noted below. The first step is to calculate the rounds per hour at the two types of tables. High yield tables have the faster dealers, specifically:

EXHIBIT 3: TYPICAL ACTIVITY TIME BREAKDOWNS

		Activity	Time Allocation (%)
EXPERT	1	Deal	55.9
	2	Shuffle	16.4
	3	Change Money	5.6
	4	Organize Chip Tray*	0.6
	5	Converse*	1.5
	6	Shift Change	20.0
			100.0
INTERMEDIATE	1	Deal	56.1
	2	Shuffle	15.9
	3	Change Money	5.9
	4	Organize Chip Tray*	1.4
	5	Converse*	0.7
	6	Shift Change	20.0
			100.0
NEOPHYTE	1	Deal	60.2
	2	Shuffle	9.7
	3	Change Money	6.8
	4	Organize Chip Tray*	0.3
	5	Converse*	3.2
	6	Shift Change	20.0
			100.0
STANDARDS	1	Deal	57.0
	2	Shuffle	15.0
	3	Change Money	6.0
	4	Organize Chip Tray*	1.0
	5	Converse*	1.0
	6	Shift Change	20.0
			100.0

* Note, these activities usually occur with dealing or shuffling, and not separately.

High-Limit Tables

0.8 [expert] × 53 rounds per hour = 42.4

0.2 [intermediate] × 40 rounds per hour = 8

Thus, there will be 50.4 rounds per hour (42.4 + 8), and the yield will be $324.07 per table per hour (50.4 × $6.43).

Low-Limit Tables

0.4 [intermediate] × 40 rounds per hour = 16

0.6 [neophyte] × 31 rounds per hour = 18.6

Thus, there will be 34.6 rounds per hour (16 + 18.6), and the yield will be $110.37 per table per hour (34.6 × $3.19).

Total revenue for the recommended method, with the same tables, is $6,516.60 per hour, for a $383.70 improvement or 6.2 percent. Consequently, the advantage of the recommended assignment of dealer to tables is $25.58 per table per hour.

Information System

The games manager should forecast the expected number of customers prior to a shift. This forecast should include a breakdown between the three types of clients. It will enable the games manager to forecast the tables needed and the high limit and low limit breakdown. In addition, the forecasts and estimates will allow the games manager to schedule dealers and forecast the expected revenue for the shift.

The feedback information should consist of actual results by number of clients, number of tables, number of dealers, and total revenue. The actuals should be compared to expectations and the differences analyzed, especially for the actual clients and revenue compared to expectations. This analysis should be used to improve forecasts and estimates for future shifts.

Conclusion

This application reveals that there is definite room for improvement with regards to staffing. With the help of management accounting, the casino can analyze its operations and deploy its resources more effectively. The recommended model showed a 6.2 percent improvement in revenues over the existing scheduling approach. This neglects the potential improvement from setting expectations for dealers as to rounds and revenue per hour.

Required Comment on how this completed project followed the project requirements.

Blind Installers

Blind Installers is an owner-managed company that installs vertical and venetian blinds, roller shades, and draperies. There are 15 employees including the owner. The following exhibit displays the functional structure. Note, the figures in brackets are the number of employees.

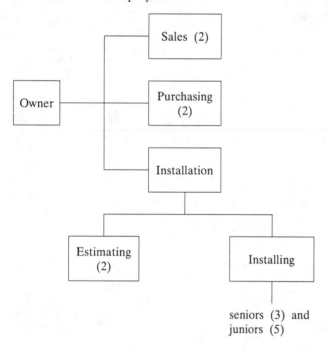

The project team analyzed the installation unit which is the major source of revenue and critical for the company's success as most sales include installation. It is only through proper installation that customers can fully appreciate their blinds.

Activities

The senior and junior installers share the activities of installing blinds and draperies. The owner directs the seniors, and the seniors in turn direct the junior installers. Seniors receive about 40 percent more an hour than juniors. A flow chart (Exhibit 1) describes the activities, clearly showing the relationship between seniors and juniors.

Detailed Description of Activities

The following describes activities in detail.

A. Two days before an installation, the owner calls the assigned senior and formally assigns the job. A senior is then responsible for ensuring that the scheduled job is done and the specified materials arrive the night before the job starts.

B. Specifications (i.e., documents such as the order, plans, etc.) arrive the night before, along with the address of the installation, window sketches and measurements, blind specifications, and requisite hardware for extraordinary windows.

C. The senior installer obtains all materials and hardware from the purchaser, who also has a copy of the specifications. Then, the senior verifies the requisite materials and hardware by doing a physical count against the specifications.

D. The purchasing department rectifies shortages.

E. The junior loads the truck with materials and tools, and replenishes the truck's standard hardware stock (screws, brackets, etc.).

F. Upon arrival at the installation site, the senior directs the junior to unload the required materials, hardware, and tools.

G. Concurrently with F, the senior places the blinds under the proper windows according to the specifications.

H. The senior drills the wall or ceiling holes for the holding brackets. The drilling requires measurement from the floor or ceiling to the

Adapted from a case by Sandro Campoli, Elena Perruzza and Stasy Presutto.

EXHIBIT 1

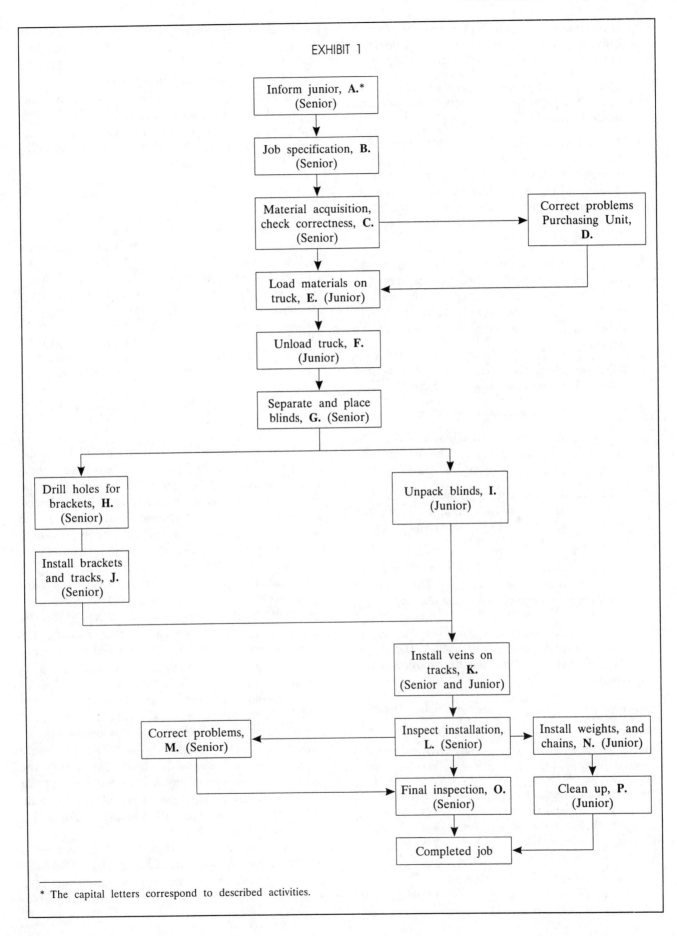

* The capital letters correspond to described activities.

hole, and the installing of a plug if needed. This allows for a firm and secure holding bracket.

I. The junior unpacks the blinds. Each has its own track packaged separately from the veins, weights, and chains.

J. Then, the junior hands a track to the senior, who clips the track to the holding bracket. Sometimes this step requires the senior to go up and down a ladder several times. Also, the senior must ensure that the track has no waves due to incorrect holding-bracket installation.

K. The junior hands the veins to the senior who stays on the ladder at one end of the track and clips them to the track. If the track is split, the senior moves with the ladder to the other end to install the second part of the veins.

L. Once installed, the senior inspects each window to ensure proper workmanship.

M. If there are problems, they are corrected.

N. As the senior inspects, the junior installs the weight on inspected veins. The weights are attached to a chain running the track length.

O. The senior conducts a final inspection to ensure that the job was completed properly and double checks for the placement of all tools in the truck.

P. Upon completion, the junior is directed to clean up the installation site. This includes removing packaging, screws, tools, etc.

When the installation is complete, the senior and junior go to the next job or back to the shop.

The following exhibit lists the grouped activities assigned to each position.

Activities	Senior	Junior	Detailed
Supervising	Yes	No	
Material acquisition	Yes	No	A,B,C,D
Loading	Yes	Yes	E,F
Separation of blinds	Yes	Yes	G,I
Drilling, bracket installation	Yes	Yes	H,J
Installing tracks and veins	Yes	Yes	J,K,L,M,O
Installing chains and weights	Yes	Yes	N
Cleaning installation site	Yes	Yes	P

Observations

Blind Installers installs many different types of blinds and draperies. The installation of verti-

cal blinds is demanding and represents most of the revenues. They are also a basis for establishing time requirements for other types of installation. The observations entailed visiting the site of five actual and representative installations that employed a senior and a junior installer. The following table shows the average time required for each aggregated activity. Exhibit 2 shows the activity time for each installation.

Activity	Average Time
Supervising	not observed
Material acquisition	1.5 minutes per unit*
Loading	1.1 minutes per unit
Separating blinds	1.2 minutes per unit
Drilling, bracket installation	0.8 minutes per foot
Installing tracks	0.3 minutes per foot
Installing veins	1.4 minutes per foot
Installing chains	1.1 minutes per foot
Installing weights	0.7 minutes per foot
Cleaning installation site	0.1 minutes per unit
and	23.0 minutes per job

* An average unit is six feet long and the average job is 50 units.

In the observations of five installations, the attachment of weights was particularly and unnecessarily awkward. After the veins are hung on the track, the junior must crouch down on his knees. He uses this position to install the weights at the bottom of each vein. This awkward position causes productivity to be lower than if the position was less awkward. Effort is minimally more if hanging occurs after attaching weights. However, this extra effort is less than the fatigue with the awkward crouched position. Thus, an alternative is for the junior to install the weights before hanging the veins. A testing of this method showed a 7 percent time saving, without considering the reduction in fatigue.

Sometimes, the senior and junior have unused time. This is because many activities are designated for senior or junior. When one was completing an activity, the other frequently had to wait before commencing a sequential activity. However, the juniors can perform many senior activities. Senior status is received after one year of employment. Often the major difference between a senior and a junior is the rate of pay.

The concern of the owner is how much work is reasonable to schedule for installers. Although installations differ in size, a crew consisting of a senior and a junior is a base for scheduling other crews.

EXHIBIT 2: OBSERVATION DETAILS

Observation	Units Per Job	Time Taken	Time Per Unit
Material acquisition			
1	15	18	1.2
2	5	9	1.8
3	25	42	1.7
4	9	10	1.1
5	3	5	1.7
Separation of blinds			
1	15	16	1.1
2	5	6	1.1
3	25	20	0.8
4	9	13	1.4
5	3	5	1.6

Observation	Feet Per Unit	Holes Per Unit	Time Taken	Time Per Foot
Drilling and bracket installation				
1	4	6	3.5	0.9
2	2	4	2.2	1.1
3	6	6	4.2	0.7
4	11	10	7.8	0.7
5	7.5	6	3.8	0.5
Installing tracks				
1	4	3	0.9	0.2
2	2	2	0.5	0.3
3	6	5	1.4	0.2
4	11	6	3.1	0.3
5	7.5	5	2.3	0.3
Installing veins				
1	4	20	5.8	1.5
2	2	10	3.2	1.6
3	6	30	8.2	1.3
4	11	55	16.4	1.5
5	7.5	38	10.2	1.4

Observation	Feet Per Unit	Veins Per Unit	Time Taken	Time Per Foot
Installing chains				
1	4	20	4.3	1.1
2	2	10	2.5	1.3
3	6	30	6.2	1.0
4	11	55	11.4	1.0
5	7.5	38	9.1	1.2
Installing weights				
1	4	20	2.5	0.6
2	2	10	1.8	0.9
3	6	30	3.7	0.6
4	11	55	7.8	0.7
5	7.5	38	6.2	0.8

Observation	Units Per Job	Time Per Unit	Time Per Job
Cleaning installation site			
1	15	4.6	28
2	5	3.3	17
3	25	5.7	37
4	9	4.0	22
5	3	3.0	12

Required With the steps to an activity costing project, complete this case by determining activity changes, establishing standards, developing an information system, and scheduling employees. Be sure to calculate the utilization rate with the scheduled employees and be sure that it is between 85 percent and 90 percent. Note: Blind Installers pays employees for 8.5 hours per day. Employees receive one hour for lunch and coffee break, which leave 7.5 hours for work.

CASE 30

Canada Savings Bonds

Located in the Toronto head office of a major brokerage firm, the unit being studied processes customer orders for Canada Savings Bonds. Generally, these bonds are sold during a two-week period in November of each year. Although this is not a highly profitable service, the brokerage firm believes it is a necessary service for its customers.

The unit consists of up to seven seconded and temporary employees during the two-week sales campaign. This includes a working manager, five data entry clerks, and one data verifier. All employees report to the manager. They are paid for 7 hours and after coffee breaks they work 6.5 hours.

Activities

The orders are generated by the branches. The unit processes these orders. In processing these orders, the manager's activities include:

- supervises the data entry clerks and the verifier,
- answers procedural questions from data entry clerks,
- wires the respective branches regarding rejected orders or the need for account numbers with new customers,
- verifies some processed orders, and makes corrections if necessary, and
- answers telephone calls from branches concerning the issue and orders.

The activities of data clerks include:

- pre-check orders to ensure correctness,
- wire the respective branches regarding rejected orders or the need for account numbers with new customers,
- process orders,
- sort confirmation sheets, i.e., one to the client, one to the sales representative, and the last to central filing, and

- clarify confusing wires by seeking advice from the manager.

The verifier does the following:

- verifies each processed order and makes changes as needed,
- files orders by number after verification.
- sends requests to the Name and Address Department for account numbers for new clients and then physically obtains those numbers, and
- answers telephone calls.

Exhibit 1 shows the activities. The letters indicate the sequence.

The matrix in Exhibit 2 shows the activities that can be done by people in each position.

Observations

Observations were conducted during the two-week campaign period. In addition, consultation and discussions were held with the manager and employees. The results listed in Exhibit 3 were the average times for each activity.

Activity Changes

There are several activity changes that the unit could implement. First, require the branches to input their own buy orders. These orders would then be verified by the unit. This would eliminate two activities, pre-checking and processing. It would also significantly reduce the chance of losing a wire and the need to wire back rejected orders. Four minutes are estimated to be the time saving per order from this activity change. However, it would require organizational decisions beyond what the manager can implement unilaterally.

Second, provide an instruction manual to each branch. The manual would outline the information required for each order and the acceptable approaches for registration. This would significantly reduce the number of telephone calls from

Adapted from a case by Hao Shen and Michael Tadros.

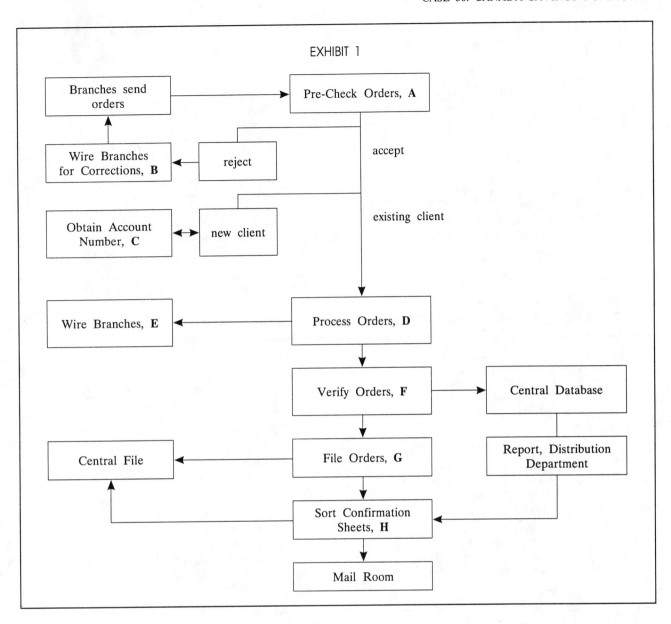

EXHIBIT 1

EXHIBIT 2

Activities	Positions		
	Manager	**Data-Entry Clerks**	**Verifier**
Asks/answers questions	yes	yes	yes
Verifies	yes	no	yes
Answers telephones	yes	yes	yes
Pre-checks	yes	yes	yes
Wires branches	yes	yes	yes
Processes orders	yes	yes	yes
Sorting	yes	yes	yes
Files	yes	yes	yes
Retrieves numbers	yes	yes	yes

EXHIBIT 3

Manager

supervises employees	90	minutes per day
answers questions	2	minutes per question
verifies	35	seconds per order
wires branches	1.5	minutes per wire

Data-Entry Clerk

pre-checks orders	35	seconds per order
processes orders	70	seconds per order
wires branches	2.5	minutes per wire
sorts confirmation sheets	70	seconds per sheet per order
asks questions of manager	2	minutes per question

Verifier

verifies	1	minute per order
files	25	seconds per order wire
retrieves account numbers	7	minutes per account number
answers telephones	4	minutes per call

EXHIBIT 4

Manager

supervises employees	60	minutes per day
answers questions	1.5	minutes per question
verifies	35	seconds per order
wires branches	1.5	minutes per wire

Data-Entry Clerk

pre-check orders	30	seconds per order
process orders	60	seconds per order
wire branches	1.5	minutes per wire
sort confirmation sheets	1	minute per sheet per order
asks questions of managers	1.5	minutes per question

Verifier

verifies	35	seconds per order
files	20	seconds per order
retrieves account numbers	5	minutes per number
answers telephones	3	minutes per call

branches as well as the number of rejected orders. It would save between three and five minutes per order.

Third, each data entry clerk could be given the answers to frequently asked questions. This will reduce the number of potential questions asked of the manager. The savings will be about three minutes per question.

Fourth, for new account numbers, the verifier spends three to four minutes going up three floors to the Name and Address Unit to submit the request. Later, he takes another three to four minutes to get the new account number. Alternative approaches (with their time savings in brackets) would be to: batch the requests (2 minutes), send fax requests (4 minutes), allow the manager to assign numbers (4.5 minutes), allow the verifier to assign numbers (4.5 minutes), and allow the data-entry clerks to assign numbers (4.5 minutes).

Establish Standards

The standards shown in Exhibit 4 are based on observations and consultation with the manager and employees. They also incorporate activity changes, particularly changes 2, 3, and the batching of requests for new account numbers.

Activity Drivers

The overwhelming activity driver is the number of orders. All activities for each position revolve around this driver. For example, the number of orders increases, the data entry clerk will ask more questions of the manager. Similarly, with more orders, there are more calls from branches. Wires to branches is also a fixed percent of the number of orders. The actual number of orders for 1993 are shown below.

Day	Orders Processed	Percentage
1	112	2.7
2	135	3.3
3	153	3.8
4	191	4.7
5	152	3.8
6	142	3.5
7	196	4.8
8	354	8.7
9	419	10.3
10	496	12.1
11	995	24.4
12	728	17.9
Total	4,073	100.0

Even after activity changes, it is expected that questions to the manager will be 30 percent of the orders until the end of day 8, then 20 percent for days 9 to 12 because of learning. Telephone calls from branches will equal 10 percent of the orders. Also, 8 percent of the orders need a wire for rejection and 2 percent for a new account number.

Required With the information provided in this case, prepare the following steps to an activity costing project: employee hour requirements, schedule employees, and information system.

Commercial Banking

Canadian banks provide many services at the branch level, broadly categorized as retail and commercial. The former represents those provided to individuals and families, while the latter are those provided to businesses. This project focuses on the commercial services, where the unit has eight employees, structured as shown below. A large portion of the unit's work entails commercial loans, and monitoring their performance.

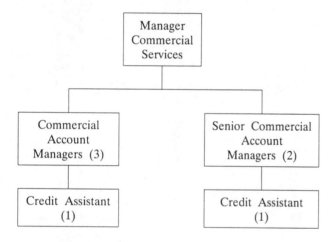

Activities

The objectives of the commercial banking unit are to make secure loans that are profitable. In achieving these objectives, the three positions have definite activities.

The activities for the manager of commercial services include:

• Oversees and directs credit activities (including preparation of credit applications, approving credits within delegated limits and recommending those in excess to ensure credit quality and effective control).

• Audits security documentation to ensure the required security is in good order and assets are adequately protected.

• Resolves customer problems and inquiries.

• Provides direction, training, counsel and performance feedback to account managers by way of performance appraisals.

• Reports periodically to the branch manager and divisional support areas in relation to strategic planning, development of effective credit control and implementation of corrective actions if necessary.

Activities of the account managers include:

• Contact and arrange appointments with existing and potential clients to discuss their requirements.

• Interview clients and review their requests.

• Prepare credit reviews as per guidelines.

• Monitor financial results and operating trends for all assigned accounts.

• Resolve customer problems and inquiries related to the accounts including both administrative and credit areas.

• Provide direction, counsel and training to support staff.

Activities of the credit assistants include:

• Maintain proper customer records for the review of account managers.

• Control files and documents for mortgages and security documentation.

• Maintain up-to-date files for non-negotiable securities.

• Assist in maintaining efficient customer service, i.e., resolves customer problems and inquiries.

• Perform sundry duties as assigned, e.g., prepares bank confirmations and general credit rating reports.

Exhibits 1 and 2 show the relationships between these activities and common, shareable activities.

Adapted from a case by Virginia Leung and Zareen Razvi.

Observations

During three weeks of observation, the activity driver was overwhelming the number of clients (or accounts). To further understand the costs generated by the unit, the team developed worked-to-time measures for each activity (Exhibit 3). Special accounts took more time than regular accounts as those clients had doubtful ability to maintain contractual payments. Not all activities depend on the number of accounts. Some are more appropriately assigned block time.

Activity Changes

The purpose of identifying activity changes is for streamlining, so that total costs will decrease.

A major problem with this unit is the excessive hours that account managers are working. They are overworked while the credit assistants have unused time. The solution is not simply a matter of giving the credit assistants more work. Clients must receive personalized attention from an account manager. However, to resolve the problem and maintain personalized attention, the account manager should invite a credit assistant to the initial interview. In this way, the credit assistant develops a relationship of trust with the client.

A major problem for the account manager is that he or she spends significant time trying to resolve customer inquiries. Credit assistants can resolve these inquiries, e.g., inquiries about the

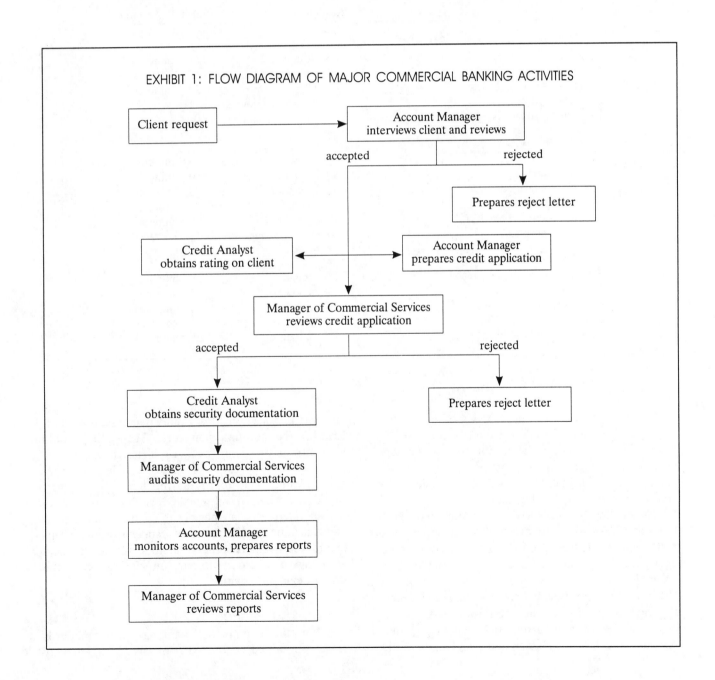

EXHIBIT 1: FLOW DIAGRAM OF MAJOR COMMERCIAL BANKING ACTIVITIES

EXHIBIT 2: COMMON ACTIVITIES AMONG POSITIONS

Activities	Manager of Commercial Services	Account Manager	Credit Assistant
Interview clients		X	X
Financial Analysis		X	X
Daily and monthly account monitoring		X	X
Resolve customer problems	X	X	X

EXHIBIT 3: ACTUAL TIMES FOR ACTIVITIES

	Regular Accounts		Special Accounts	
Manager of commercial services				
Oversees credit preparation	25	minutes	60	minutes
Audits documentation	5	minutes	15	minutes
Resolves client problems	—		20	minutes
Counsels and trains	35 minutes per day			
Reports to superiors	60 minutes per day			
Account managers				
Contact clients	3	minutes	3	minutes
Interview clients	30	minutes	50	minutes
Prepare applications	150	minutes	360	minutes
Monitoring	6	minutes	20	minutes
Resolve client problems	10	minutes	25	minutes
Trains support staff	15 minutes per day			
Credit assistants				
Prepare and maintains records	15	minutes	20	minutes
Control securities	5	minutes	5	minutes
Maintain files	10	minutes	15	minutes
Sundry	8	minutes	15	minutes
Resolve client problems	15	minutes	25	minutes

current loan balance or the amount of loan interest paid. A better procedure would be to have the client call the credit assistant for routine matters, and then if necessary, contact the account manager. This arrangement can only be feasible if the credit assistant knows the client.

Generally, 80 percent of an account manager's time should be used to prepare credit applications and reviews. However, much of the account manager's time is spent on more routine, simple tasks. Examples are writing to and following up with the client for current financial information and updating the first portion of the application. If the credit assistant obtains the current financial information, prepares the spreadsheet analysis, and updates the

current data section, this would decrease the workload of the account managers. Again, they could concentrate on their specialized functions.

Another suggestion involves problem or special accounts that represent much of the account managers' time. If all of the problem loans were consolidated into a special unit, this would allow centralization and promote specialization. This would economize on the total time needed to deal with lawyers, etc., without interfering with the unit's regular activities.

Establish Standards

For the commercial banking unit, standards were developed based on observations, activity

EXHIBIT 4: STANDARD TIMES FOR ACTIVITIES

	Regular Accounts		Special Accounts	
Manager of commercial services				
Oversees preparation of credits	20	minutes	45	minutes
Audits security documentation	5	minutes	10	minutes
Resolves customer problems	—		10	minutes
Account managers				
Contact clients	3	minutes	3	minutes
Interview clients	30	minutes	45	minutes
Prepare applications	120	minutes	300	minutes
Monitoring	4	minutes	15	minutes
Resolve customer problems	6	minutes	20	minutes
Credit assistants				
Prepare client records	12	minutes	15	minutes
Control securities	5	minutes	5	minutes
Maintain files	8	minutes	10	minutes
Sundry	5	minutes	10	minutes
Resolve client problems	10	minutes	20	minutes

changes, and in consultation with the manager of commercial services and other employees. These standards represent the time spent on each customer or account.

It is important to take the effects of the learning curve into account. Here the learning curve would predict that the time per customer decreases as the number of served customers increases. The eight employees have been with the unit for over a year. Most are close to the point where learning is no longer a major factor. Thus, the currently attainable standards were developed considering the current level of expertise and knowledge possessed by the employees (see Exhibit 4).

Activity Drivers

The number of accounts or clients is the activity driver. Total accounts are convertible to accounts per day, assuming 47 weeks a year. Where the actual yearly data were unavailable, the manager and other employees made estimates. There were no peak client periods during the week or the year. The only annual fluctuations were that business was usually slower during the summer and in December when many clients were on vacation. Account managers observed that the mornings were busier than the afternoons, since this is the time they performed their account monitoring by reviewing daily reports (see Exhibit 5).

Employee Hour Requirements

The employee hour requirements were for an average day, i.e., daily volumes times the standard time for each activity, and then totalled for each position. Required hours divided by seven hours yielded the utilization rate. The seven hours was the seven and a half hours paid, less two 15-minute coffee breaks. This was the total time available from paid time less two paid coffee breaks.

Accordingly, the manager of commercial services would work 358 minutes a day (5.97 hours) for a utilization rate of 85.3 percent. The account managers would work 477 minutes (7.94 hours) for 113.4 percent utilization. Meanwhile, for those average days, the credit assistants would work 346 minutes (5.8 hours) for a utilization rate of 82.3 percent.

Information System

For the annual budget, the manager of commercial services must forecast the expected number of client accounts by type and get agreement on time standards for the accomplishment of that work. Specifically, that would entail forecasts for all volumes in Exhibit 5. It would also include agreement on the standard time per activity.

The manager of commercial services would schedule staff based on the forecasts and standards, which would comprise a budget at the activity level. With monthly comparison of actual to budget,

EXHIBIT 5: ACTIVITY VOLUME

	Yearly Accounts		Daily Accounts	
	Regular	Special	Regular	Special
Manager of commercial services				
Oversees credit	895	680	3.8	2.9
Audits documentation	895	680	3.8	2.9
Resolves client problems	—	200	—	0.9
Account managers				
Contact clients	235	38	1.0	0.2
Interview clients	210	25	0.9	0.1
Prepare applications	185	18	0.8	0.1
Monitoring	11,500	1,000	49.0	4.3
Resolve customer problems	1,400	138	6.0	0.6
Credit assistants				
Prepare client records	2,025	780	8.6	3.3
Control securities	1,100	350	4.7	1.5
Maintain files	1,810	850	7.7	3.6
Sundry	900	175	3.8	0.7
Resolve client problems	705	85	3.0	0.4

variance analysis can be done. In effect, this would be a flexible budget which adjusts to changes in the activity driver (e.g., the number of accounts) since the environment is uncertain. The budget should not be rigid and should consider the fact that a change in conditions, e.g., economic, requires a change in plans. Actual clients' accounts and other volume data already exist in bank data bases.

Schedule Employees

In considering employee hour requirements, the manager of commercial services is being underutilized. The time required for his activities amounts to only about 6 hours per day. However, instead of taking on the work of the account managers or credit assistants, perhaps his free time could go to account growth and employee monitoring.

The employee hour requirement schedule also shows that the account managers are being over utilized. Their workload would require about 7 hours and 56 minutes for each account manager. They work about 56 minutes a day more than full utilization. Since there are five account managers, the total work overload is about 4.7 hours.

The credit assistants can do some routine activities (refer to Exhibit 2) of the account managers, such as interviewing clients, account monitoring, financial analysis, and resolving customer problems. The most effective way for them to help would be to do some account monitoring, which is done during the peak volume period and is the one activity that requires the most time. They can also screen customer calls and gather information on customers for credit applications. Even with the assignment of credit assistants to account manager activities, their available time is insufficient to cover the 5-hour shortage. Thus, there is still an overload of 2.5 hours a day. A suggestion is to hire a part-time employee to do the routine functions of credit assistants, so that they can assist with the account monitoring. These changes will help this unit achieve a reasonable utilization rate.

Required Note how the case has followed the project requirements. Be sure to evaluate the activity changes.

Mexican Fine and Fast Foods

Mexican Fine and Fast Foods (FFF) is a popular restaurant chain serving modestly priced Mexican food in clean and comfortable combination eat-in and take-out facilities. The particular subject of this case is a typical unit with 25 full- and part-time employees. The employees are grouped into three positions: the unit manager, assistant manager, and crew member. The manager is responsible for complete operations within the guidelines established by his supervisor, the market manager. Only the manager and assistant manager have full-time positions. The remaining employees are employed as needed. The physical layout is shown in Exhibit 1.

Activities

The activities to be accomplished by staff in each position are specified below.

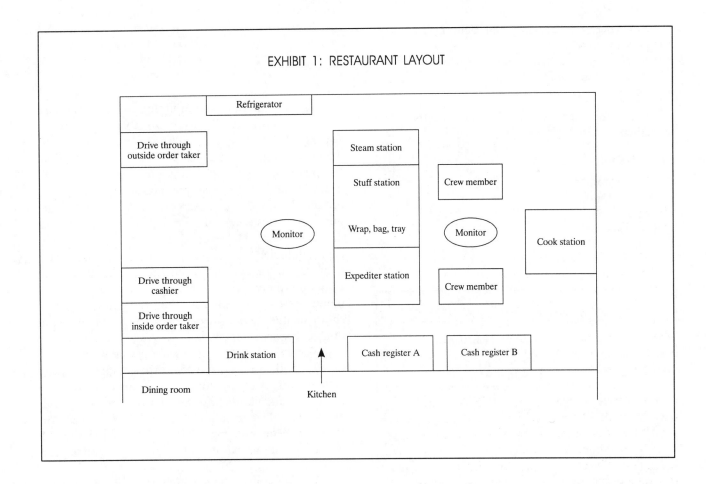

EXHIBIT 1: RESTAURANT LAYOUT

Adapted from a case by Gigi Fung, Ken Le and Kenneth Lun.

Unit Manager

- serve customers and deliver food when the restaurant is busy,
- supervise crew members,
- tend to administrative responsibilities,
- schedule crew members,
- prepare performance reports, and
- recruit new employees.

The manager's administrative duties include payroll preparation, ensuring compliance with government regulations, benefits administration, budget preparation, cost control, and bank deposits.

The assistant manager has activities similar to the manager. Administration duties include those not done by the unit manager. As well, part of the assistant manager's time goes to serving customers while ensuring that crew members are performing their requisite activities. The assistant manager, and the unit manager, work eight hour shifts.

Assistant Manager

- serve customers, prepare and deliver food,
- supervise crew members,
- tend to administrative duties,
- schedule crew members, and
- train crew members.

Crew members work five hour shifts when scheduled.

Crew Member

- serve customers,
- prepare food,
- deliver food,
- clean, and
- stock.

EXHIBIT 2: POSITIONS AND ACTIVITIES

	Positions		
Activities	**Crew Member**	**Assistant Manager**	**Unit Manager**
Serve customers	Yes	Yes	Yes
Prepare food	Yes	Yes	Yes
Deliver food	Yes	Yes	Yes
Clean	Yes	Yes	Yes
Stock	Yes	Yes	Yes
Supervise	No	Yes	Yes
Administration	No	Yes	Yes
Schedule	No	Yes	Yes
Train	No	Yes	Yes
Performance report	No	No	Yes
Recruit	No	No	Yes

Exhibit 2 relates activities performed in the unit to staff able to perform them. This suggests opportunities for assigning activities to different staff members to make the best use of employee costs.

Observations

Activity times came from observations and asking questions about employee time requirements. There is an activity driver — number of orders — for many activities, but others have to be done despite the number of orders.

Activity	Actual Time Requirements	
Serve customers	30	seconds per order
Prepare food	30	seconds per order
Deliver food	5	seconds per order
Clean	20	minutes per day
Stock	15	minutes per day
Supervise	4	hours per day
Administration	9.5	hours per day
Schedule	60	minutes per day
Train	30	minutes per day
Performance report	60	minutes per day
Recruit	60	minutes per day

The actual time required for an activity does not necessarily imply a reasonable attainment. During the observations, there were three crew members working in the preparation area. Two computer monitors recorded orders from cash registers, A and B. Six was the maximum number of orders displayed on a screen, which limited the number of customers. For most of the day this is not a problem. However, during peak periods this capacity limits the serving of customers and leads to many customers waiting to order. This is unnecessary as there is a second unused line with two monitors to the left of the preparation table, shown in the kitchen layout. The second line could double capacity.

The manager does not schedule crew members based on the day's expected orders which is predictable. By not scheduling to expected orders, there are not necessarily the appropriate scheduled employees. This results in some actual times for activities being too high. Consequently, the revised standard for preparing food is 15 seconds per order down from 30.

In addition, the manager has an opportunity to explicitly direct the activities of crew members. This is a particular problem with cleaning which gets less time than required. Also, there is difficulty in explaining "clean." In this regard, a consultant recently hired by the parent organization

EXHIBIT 3: ORDERS DURING DAY		
	Number of Orders	
Hours of Operation	Normal Weather Conditions	Unfavourable Weather Conditions
10:00–11:00	1	0
11:01–12:00	27	15
12:01–1:00	63	64
1:01–2:00	66	76
2:01–3:00	27	13
3:01–4:00	24	7
4:01–5:00	29	25
5:01–6:00	42	30
6:01–7:00	61	37
7:01–8:00	51	28
8:01–9:00	38	20
9:01–10:00	23	12
10:01–11:00	7	3
11:01–11:30	3	0
Total	462	330

reviewed the unit's hospitality, quality, service, and cleanliness. The standard is 95 percent, but this

unit scored only 93 percent. This poor performance reduced the manager's bonus. Insufficient cleaning was the cause of these shortcomings. For example, the consultant noted that there were trays and food packaging on unoccupied tables. The seating areas and floors were dirty. The garbage containers were full and the rest rooms were filthy.

Cost Drivers

A common denominator for the selling activity at a Mexican FFF unit is the average order. Although orders vary in dollar size and the time required to complete, an average order is a valid means for planning and executing workloads.

There is a marked variation in orders per hour during an average day. This pattern changes with the weather. Exhibit 3 notes these variations for different hours of the day.

Required Complete this case with the following steps: activity changes, standards, employee hour requirements, information system, and scheduling employees. Be sure to calculate the utilization rate of the scheduled employees and be sure that it is between 80 and 90 percent.

Protectco

Protectco is a medium-sized security firm serving the greater metropolitan Toronto area. This study focuses on the municipal law enforcement division, which is comprised of:

- a divisional supervisor,
- three full-time and three part-time municipal law enforcement officers (MLEO), and
- two full-time assistants who acquire contracts and perform administrative duties.

All employees report to the supervisor, who reports to the general manager of Protectco. The division's mandate is to provide clients with a law enforcement service that cannot be adequately provided by regular police forces. All MLEOs are certified under the police services act to enforce municipal bylaws.

Activities

Clients hire the division to enforce municipal bylaws on their properties. This is accomplished mainly by issuing parking infraction notices (tags) to vehicles illegally parked on client property. This tagging service is augmented by site inspections and surveillance to produce a comprehensive enforcement package.

The following activities comprise the work of the division:

Supervisor

- responds to client inquiries and complaints,
- monitors subordinates, including the arrangement of staff meetings and the review of daily MLEO reports,
- schedules employees,
- gathers information, which includes attending Metro Council meetings for updates and changes to all municipal bylaws, and obtaining legal advice,

- obtains contracts, i.e., submits tenders, solicits new business by telephone, and reviews current contracts, and
- finalizes contracts, i.e., negotiates contract terms and conditions.

Assistants

- responds to client inquiries and complaints,
- obtains contracts,
- finalizes contracts,
- maintains books and performs clerical duties i.e., filing and telephone reception duties.

MLEOs

- issue tags, i.e., parking infraction notices to illegally parked vehicles,
- inspect client sites,
- survey client premises for theft, illegal dumping, etc.

MLEO activities can be divided into sub-activities. Parking tickets are issued to vehicles illegally parked. When this involves a timed zone, a chalk mark will be placed against a tire to assist in measuring the time violation. If the vehicles are in a tow-away zone, they will be tagged and a tow truck will be called to tow them to a compound. Inspections involve observing the exterior of a client's premises for forced entry. If there has been forced entry, the local police are called, the client is informed, and the premises are secured. An interior inspection is done simultaneously. Surveillance is similar to inspections, except that a premise is observed for a certain unacceptable activity.

All major activities have been cross-referenced on the activity matrix (Exhibit 1) to show the relationship with positions. This matrix assists with scheduling and encourages cross training to increase scheduling flexibility. The letter P indicates the

Adapted from a case by Gary Kopriva and Gurjit Saluja.

EXHIBIT 1: ACTIVITY MATRIX

	Supervisor	MLEO	Assistants
Respond to inquiries	P		P
Monitors subordinates	P		
Schedules	P		C
Gathers information	P		C
Obtains contracts	P		P
Finalizes contracts	P		P
Maintains books, etc.	C		P
Issues tags	C	P	
Inspects	C	P	
Surveys	C	P	

---

activities performed by staff in each position, while C connotes activities each employee can also do.

Observations

Work-to-time relationships were identified for each activity. They were based on observations during two days and are presented in Exhibit 2.

Some activities rarely occur, e.g., calling the police, making an arrest, and informing clients. When they do, the client is billed for the additional time.

Activity Changes

A major obstacle to streamlining is that the activities of the division are strictly governed by contractual obligations and legal parameters. For example, when inspecting the exterior of a building, the contract specifies that all doors and ground level windows must be checked by hand to ensure the premises are secure. Deviating from this requirement would jeopardize the contract and could result in legal repercussions should the officer fail to secure the premises. During tagging, the Police Services Act requires that in the spirit of justice, all tags must be written "painstakingly accurate" to ensure the system is equitably applied. The issuance of incorrect tags can lead to the decertification of an officer.

Within these constraints, it was realized that the MLEOs spend considerable time writing long site inspection reports that said the same thing each time. The format of these reports was not bound by contractual obligations or legal parameters. A proposed standardized report format for site inspections was developed and submitted to the supervisor for a trial run. The result of the trial run was to virtually eliminate the time spent on writing reports. This reporting format was subsequently adopted by Protectco. Appendix 1 is a sample of the reporting format.

There is a delay when waiting for a tow truck. Typically, a tow truck operator is called after the discovery of a towable vehicle. Instead, the tow truck can be waiting at the site when the MLEO arrives. The tow truck would be waiting somewhere anyway, and this coordination would reduce the time for the MLEO and the operator.

Standards

Protectco is remunerated by clients at negotiated rates. Tagging receives 90 minutes per site visit while inspection and surveillance receive 60 and 190 minutes, respectively. The total billed time for a recent day is summarized in the following table.

Time Billed by MLEOs

Major Activities	MLEO					
	1	2	3	4	5	6
Tagging at 90 minutes	180	360	180	270	180	0
Inspection at 60 minutes	240	240	240	0	120	0
Surveillance at 90 minutes	180	90	270	0	0	360
Daily billed by MLEO	600	690	690	270	300	360

Total charged for day, 2,910 minutes or 48.5 hours.

Based on observations and activity changes, standard times are used in the following table. They are 45 minutes for tagging, 30 minutes for inspection, and 84 minutes for surveillance.

EXHIBIT 2

SUPERVISOR Activities	Actual Time Observed	
responds to inquiries	20	minutes per day
monitors subordinates	60	minutes per day
schedules	30	minutes per day
gathers information	170	minutes per day
obtains contracts	50	minutes per day
finalizes contracts	60	minutes per day
Total time spent per day	390	minutes or 6.5 hours

ASSISTANTS Activities	Actual Time Observed	
responds to inquiries	30	minutes per day
obtains contracts	240	minutes per day
finalizes contracts	30	minutes per day
maintains books, clerical	120	minutes per day
Total time spent per day	420	minutes or 7 hours

MLEO Activities	Actual Tagging Times in Minutes			
Sub-activity	Site 1	Site 2	Site 3	Site 4
Travel	16	18	22	14
Inspect/chalk	15	11	11	19
Tag	0	0	5	9
Tag and tow	19	33	28	0
Total	50	62	66	42

Average time per site = 55 minutes.

	Actual Inspection Time in Minutes			
Sub-activity	Site 1	Site 2	Site 3	Site 4
Travel	12	16	12	17
Inspect exterior	9	5	4	8
Inspect interior	8	6	7	19
Call police/arrest	0	0	0	0
Inform client	0	0	0	0
Secure premises	0	0	0	0
Write report	7	4	4	6
Total	36	31	27	50

Average time per site = 36 minutes.

	Actual Surveillance Time in Minutes	
Sub-activity	Time Spent	
Travel	17	minutes
Observations	65	
Call police/arrest	0	
Inform client	0	
Write report	7	
Total	89	minutes

Standard Time by MLEOs

	MLEO					
Major Activities	**1**	**2**	**3**	**4**	**5**	**6**
Tagging at 45 minutes	90	180	90	135	90	0
Inspection at 30 minutes	120	120	120	0	60	0
Surveillance at 84 minutes	168	84	252	0	0	336
Daily required by MLEO	378	384	462	135	150	336

Total charged for day, 1845 minutes or 30.75 hours.

Standard time is substantially lower than chargeable time by 1,065 minutes.

Activity Drivers

One activity driver is prevalent. It is the number of site visits. As contracts are generally for a month, the number of active contracts fluctuates monthly. July and August are the slowest months. The following table shows the contracts for the past year.

Month	Active Contracts
January	25
February	24
March	26
April	26
May	26
June	21
July	16
August	15
September	22
October	24
November	24
December	27

The number of daily site visits varies according to contracts. The following schedule is an example of site visits during a recent day.

Distribution of Site Visits

Time	Parking	Inspection	Surveillance	Total
8 am–12 pm	5	1	0	6
12 pm–4 pm	2	3	0	5
4 pm–8 pm	1	2	2	5
8 pm–12 am	3	3	3	9
12 am–4 am	1	3	3	7
4 am–8 am	1	2	2	5

Employee Hour Requirements

The supervisor's hour requirement for an average day is 390 minutes or 6.5 hours. With 8 hours in his day, less 30 minutes for two coffee breaks, the available time is 7.5 hours. Thus, his utilization rate is 86.7 percent (6.5/7.5). This utilization rate allows time for one site visit a day. The assistants each work 7 hours of an available 7.5 hours for 93.3 percent utilization. They have no time available for site visits. Site visits are assigned to the full-time MLEOs first, and then to the part-time MLEOs as there is work available. Full-time MLEOs work 40 hours a week.

With the standard time requirements for the above set of site visits, the following employee hour requirements are needed for the respective time slots.

Employee Hour Requirements

Time	Parking	Inspection	Surveillance	Total
8 am–12 pm	225	30	0	255
12 pm–4 pm	90	90	0	180
4 pm–8 pm	45	60	168	273
8 pm–12 am	135	90	252	477
12 am–4 am	45	90	252	387
4 am–8 am	45	60	168	273
				1,845

In total 1,845 minutes or 30.75 hours is required for the above recent day.

Required Schedule employees, calculate their utilization rates, and prepare an information system for managing the employee scheduling.

APPENDIX 1

Protectco Limited

PATROL INSPECTION REPORT

Client _____

Location _____

Date _____ Time in _____ Time out _____

Inspection officer _____

Exterior check list		**Interior check list**	
Exit doors	☐	Doors	☐
Windows	☐	Windows	☐
Lighting	☐	Secured areas	☐
Fire route	☐	Stairwells	☐
Garbage	☐	Lighting	☐
Parking lot	☐	Equipment running	☐
Fencing	☐	Fire equipment	☐
Perimeter gates	☐	Fire alarm points	☐
Equipment running	☐	Sprinkler pressure	☐
Vehicles on location	☐	Unauthorized persons	☐
Other (explain)	☐	Other (explain)	☐

_____

_____

_____

_____

Original left on site?   Yes _____ No _____.

Complete this form in duplicate _____

(signature of inspecting officer)